THE 52 MAGIC LAWS

Olivier Honsperger

The 52 Magic Laws

The secrets of life

Second edition

Magic Laws

The author of this book does not give any medical advice, the information contained in this book is for educational purposes and should not be used to diagnose, replace a consultation with a health care professional or write a prescription in order to solve a health problem. He simply wants to provide general information that can help anyone in his or her search for emotional and spiritual well-being. The author and publisher shall in no case be liable for misuse of this information.

Editing&   Translation: Nicolas Kuhn, Revision: Michelle Macdonald
Photo: Sophie Burki

1st edition / March 2013
2nd edition / October 2013

Copyright n° 25 1 15 21 8 23 by Olivier Honsperger
ISBN: Soft cover 978-2-9544710-2-0
Printed in the United States of America: December 2013
Legal deposit fourth quarter of 2013
Library of Congress

Magic Laws Publishing
2 rue Voltaire – Case postale 1083
CH 1211 Genève 1
Switzerland
www.magiclaws.com

"Nothing can make us happier
than making someone else happy."

"Whatever you can do or dream you can, begin it.
Boldness has genius, power and magic in it!"

Johann Wolfgang Von GOETHE

PREFACE

Throughout history men have sought the secret of life and of the Universe.

Prehistoric men were the first to draft the first notions of art and metaphysics in their paintings on the walls of their protective caverns.

Later philosophers have tried as well; greeks and romans, and after them, old sages in western Europe and the Orient.

Then came scientists and prophets in Europe, like Nostradamus, Galileo, Copernicus and Giordano Bruno; the templar knights also followed this quest. And of course the sadhus of India, the Mayas and all the shamans around the world.

The answers offered by the sages were mostly theoretical or transcendental and only a few of them offered a way of life.

This book is not intended to give an answer, but it offers a way to answer to oneself.

What are you doing for this existence, which has been offered to you, to be really your life, a rich and fulfilling life?

How are you really going to make further progress in your life? Or even transform it?

Here are some elements that will help you to understand that you are truly in presence of an exceptional way to improve your life.

The two key virtues of your transformation are daily **Progression** and **Practice**. This book offers more a practical approach than a theoretical one.

It is true that theories fail when it comes to changing one's own life. It is nothing less than to choosing to take charge of one's life through a simple and regular practice to create a beautiful life for oneself.

Despite the legitimate interest that one may have in teachings of oriental and western philosophies, certainly not negligible, one must admit that it only concerns the field of ideas. But the true philosophy is to live your ideas, is it not?

The true role of this book is to help you change your lifestyle in daily life and in your very own existence.

To become the ideal person you aspire to be, you need to undergo an essential transformation of your behavior in the world, whether you are alone or with others, the way you think, the way you see yourself and people in your circle.

Human progress, your progress in life, entails inexorably transforming yourself, a kind of mental and physical gymnastics.

You just have to take care of yourself, to be fully yourself, like adhering to the words that John Lennon sang, *"Just believe in You."*

You just have **to experiment** every day with simple exercises that you will have fun completing.

This way **you learn to live your life**, and to live becomes a verb in active mode. You just need to allow yourself to enjoy the new pleasures of life you are going to discover. Everything will easily fit into place.

Because it is about being better, taking care of oneself and making every moment pleasant, just like when we are in love. Take real care of yourself and offer yourself happiness and joy as gifts owed to you.

What is the origin of the fundamental law?

We all know the law of universal gravitation, which governs the planetary movements. We know that in the microcosm the particles move with a clean energy.

Today we know that we send information to each other through pheromone secretions or through magnetic waves induced by electrical transmission of brain activity. To these information modes are added gestures or less visible signs, such as changes in sweating or pupillary movements. But if we take for granted the law of attraction that can move huge stars, it is easy to conceive a law of attraction that interconnects living beings by making them interact. You should know that the law of the laws is the one of attraction and the law of compensation is one of its major components that will be discussed later on.

Among all the laws the one of resonance is the simplest law and the most difficult to incorporate in our life. This is the only law that has been banned from sacred writings by the religious leaders or the people in charge of the community. One may wonder what would justify such a stubbornness not to let humanity apply this fundamental law. This is obviously because this law gives us power!

The power that allow you to create the life you want. Of course it seems impossible at first, for the simple reason that we are somehow programmed and formatted by our education or our beliefs and led to believe that this cannot be done.

However, for a hundred years many researchers, philosophers and great writers have struggled to retrieve and transcribe the original sacred writings and to understand some of their applications. The secret of the universal application of the law of attraction lies deep within our brains. Millions of neurologic sensors emit waves far beyond our physical body as do radio waves.

Great scientists and inventors such as Einstein or Edison knew this very well, and many of their writings refer to this phenomenon. Our brain has indeed the unique ability to transmit and receive, without any limitation in space. Every thought you have forms a wave emitted around you that projects outwardly to the universe and ends up materializing (more and more quickly). Chekhov said:

"We literally are what we think."

If you had to remember only one formula, it would be this: **"You become what you think about most often."** (Earl Nightingale)

The Law of Attraction is the most powerful law and the hardest to apply in one's life. It is especially the most difficult to accept because it goes against many teachings anchored in our minds over the years. And yet it will be necessary to become aware of the influence of all the beliefs that hinder clear and positive application of this law. What you currently are is the result of your thoughts. It is your thoughts that led to the position where you are at that precise moment.

You are solely responsible for your life. External influences can certainly change the course of some events, but they are relatively minor compared to the influence you can exert by yourself, with the power of your thoughts. The law of attraction is like a magnet: neither good nor evil, no notions of fair or unfair. It "is" just like the air we breathe. You attract the experiences and relationships that you think about the most often.

One's just need to change his/her way of thinking to permanently change one's future… it may sound too good to be true, and yet it is so.

The implementation of this change, as obvious as it looks, is not that easy. The purpose of this book is precisely to guide you to succeed in implementing these desired changes. We always have the possibility to read books on the subject, or to undergo training in this field. But this does not cause any change in our lives if we do not immediately apply the information learnt.

Intellectual knowledge of this force remains a concept lurking in a part of our brain and will generate only very little change. On the contrary, the practical application of it activates neuronal activity using the areas of the brain dedicated to feelings that are also the ones of creativity. Think back to your different experiences of life: *every time you really wanted something with your gut and your senses, you have, most of the time, obtained it.*

In contrast, a more cerebral thought, not really felt, so not really desired, is not followed by any effect. The experience shape your belief, yours, not that of another, nor even the one mentioned by any dogma.

We could go further to say: do not believe what you read in this book. But **have faith in your own belief** that you build by putting it into practice. The law of compensation is a fundamental law developed by all religions and ancient philosophies. When one really assimilates it, it becomes impossible to say to oneself:
I am unlucky; otherwise why are all these problems, all these troubles happening to me?
Some call it Karma, others the law of cause and effect. But there is no need to seek the reasons for what is going wrong in a more or less traumatic past, in the life of our ancestors or in any external cause.

It is what we thought and planted, here, in the present moment, that we harvest.

If we turn our attention to misery, revolt or fight, then we will live our life in the difficulties and ongoing conflict.

If instead we focus our daily attention only on positive elements, if we give and share, while being at peace in our minds, we will receive benefits profusely in our life.

This page is left intentionnaly blank.

WHY THIS BOOK?

For nearly twenty years I have been teaching the basics of personal development through training courses that I ran or books I have published, and yet it is very recently that I finally understood **the real secret.**

At times, in situation in my personal life that did not agree with me, I would recharge my batteries by reading my own writing, my own books. It is the paradox of the poorly shod shoemaker stretched to the limit, I thought: *no, this is impossible, did I write that?*

Actually, like most of us, we apply too little of what we learn for things to really change. Since this new awareness, I decided to gather the best ideas of my teachings, writings, lectures, thinking or exercises, as well as all the contributions from philosophy and science, to make a compilation of the best of best with its real-world application.

As I mentioned earlier, for a change of life to be possible, **one has to be willing to apply this teaching in his/her day-to-day life,** otherwise nothing happens.

I finally decided to apply 100% of what I had learnt, wrote and taught.

Thus, during my transcribing work to formulate and develop each of these laws, I realized that a new dimension emanated from me, a new force, an intense peace, joy to be able to be happy no matter what happens, the possibility of what I can have, be or become. I thought: but it works!

The more I wrote, the more I fine-tuned the writing of this new book, the more I was excited and my life and my dreams became beautiful. Sometimes when what I expected from life was slow to come about and impatience took over, I plunged back into my manuscript and reread to see what law I could have missed in order to apply it in the course of my personal life. And each time, I discovered the answer, my life regained its energy and I got my enthusiasm back. I could then immediately resume my work with a brand new freshness. And this is how, thanks to of all these experiences, I really understood the power of these concepts and the corresponding exercises. I have of course, them myself, applied assiduously and enjoyed what they produced in my life.

My deepest desire is to share these lessons with the largest number of people through this book. For now I know that if these magic laws and formulas are applied, it is possible to live our life at every moment, with depth and intensity.

Illness, health, misfortune, happiness, poverty, wealth appear only as beliefs, ways of thinking, nothing is true!

Change your beliefs and you will change your reality!

INSTRUCTIONS

The book is divided into four sections of twelve weeks and includes a final section of four weeks. Each component is a step with specific subjects to assimilate at a certain pace.

After each step, you will see significant progress in your life, **investing only three to five minutes a day.**

You can easily perceive this transformation, if of course you assiduously put into practice the applications presented in this book and if you carefully follow these instructions.

This is a book that appeals to the heart, so naturally you have to learn *by heart* the essential phrases to make them a permanent part of yourself and of your lifestyle.

Each phrase, motto, explanation and practice has been specially designed to have a direct impact, which allows you to assimilate and integrate each law.

Each week, a new law (and therefore a new theme) will be presented so that you can make it your own.

So you should carry with you all the time, texts regarding this law during the current week, and you use it as a vade-mecum (a reference manual you carry around).

Focus all your attention on the page of the law and its applications at least **once every hour, every day.**

This way of practicing (modus operandi), repetitive and methodical is the only way to obtain a successful outcome.

It is also a good idea to get a small notebook to write down the exercises and practices to do.

You have to read, re-read and understand the meaning and

implications of these laws. You will then find out, from your practical experience, that these lessons have been anchored in your true beliefs and become indestructible.

The results will bring you intense joy; it will then be impossible for you to go back.

If you do what you have always done, you will get what you always got.

How could you imagine for one second otherwise?

If you want things to change, you must first change things yourself and things will change.

THE 52 LAWS

With the help of these laws, you will establish your personal code, like no other, because it is only effective for your personality, your own feelings and your experiences.

Under these unified laws of your personal code, therein lies your secret, your treasure.

They will guide every act, every thought, and every decision at every moment of your life.

They will **become your Reason to live and your Lifestyle**. This means your strictly personal way to experience life and live it with your own feelings. These laws are each associated with guide-phrases: motto, dictum or quote that you can easily learn and take ownership of. You can refer to them, without difficulty, in every important moment of your life. These laws and mottos, you can meditate on and think about because they are the ones that guide your life. From immemorial time, people have referred to talisman phrases that were used for their meditations and prayers. The power of your code, maxims and laws that make up your art of living lies not only in their meaning, although it fundamentally represents what you are. These laws are also a support, as you can recite them to yourself. You can repeat the mantra mentally, singing with your inner voice. Why not, indeed, chanting, as it has been known for centuries and all religions have indulged in this, that to repeat phrases continually plunges us into a state of relaxation and concentration that makes us able to do the toughest jobs and put us in a state of mind that is unequalled. We retrieve these almost hypnotic verbalizations in Christian prayer as well as in the Talmudic chanting, singing of muezzins or reciting of Buddhist sutras. However, these religious meditations are made from texts that are not understandable since they are often recited in a language (ancient or extinct) that is not understood. The Buddhists in Japan, for example, mumble sutras of ancient Indian language, which, moreover, had to be phonetically transcribed to be pronounceable in Japanese and easily remembered.

On the contrary, your secret code is formulated in your own language and exactly matches what you are and your course of life. Life has not been given to you by chance and you will choose with your secret code to live it freely and to give it the value that you will have yourself estimated. What you just need to remember, no need to have had a university education, is the *Hic and Nunc* meaning "here and now" and *Carpe Diem* inviting simply to seize the day. This book, with a huge ambition, but a lot of modesty as it is about the self responds to an aspiration that concerns all of us.

It is your own code, which like all codes is a collection of laws. It includes fifty-two vital laws and highlights ten key laws you will choose, not as obligations, such as those of the Ten Commandments of the Bible, but as necessities.

It is not about concepts, but about experiences to live. You can easily perform the exercises every day, at every moment, so they are not exercises anymore, but become your lifestyle. Enjoying the happiness of your new life, thanking again for this delicious gift, give... Give to your loved ones the opportunity to get what you will be able to achieve and become, by sharing and living these magic laws.

To start each day, here is this sentence to read every morning.

Today.......... is a very important day...

Because I have DECIDED:
- that nothing will impede this wonderful day, I focus on positive thoughts, that please me, those where I feel well;
- today to attract only experiences of joy, lightness and love; we do not care about the rest!

> "To kill a man,
> simply prevent him from dreaming."
>
> ALLAN D. LEBKOY

The dream breakers: leave them in the nightmares of others!

The dream is the only way to color the Black and White of life. Fix your dream machine! Dream big! Dream often! But **Dream!**

Never let anyone convince you that your dreams are too big. The dream is the only path that builds the highways of life, which gives hope to life when we believe that life has no meaning and no way out.

Your dream, the one you have always had inside you since you are able to think, the one that will go further than others can imagine, follow it. Let yourself be carried away by it. It is the powerful and magnificent torrent that drives your life.

Not everyone will listen your story, the one of your dream: it does not matter. They do not have the same vision as you do. But what is really important:

Never accept the dream or the story of others.

Keep yours, always: do not change your course!

The greatness of your being is shaped by the size of your dreams.

Practice

The exercise of this first week is to make your book of dreams. Dare writing anything that makes you dream, review this book every morning, until your dreams come true...

Never stop, if we do not dream anymore we die.

Make a first list of the top ten subjects that make you dream the most, starting with those that seem most realistic.

This will encourage you to see all of your dreams gradually come true one by one. There are no taboo, no censorship to apply. These are your dreams, they concern no one else and they motivate your life: so there shall be no limit.

Write as if you had already achieved your dreams and fully received from life, and thanking for this gift.

"This house is my own and here I dwell, I have never aped nothing from one and – laugh at each master, mark me well, who at himself has not poked fun."

FRIEDRICH NIETZSCHE

Laugh and smile every day; this way life smiles at you.

A smile is an exterior sign of inner wealth. It is a universal language, regardless of age or culture.

A laugh is a direct route to the soul.

The more we advance in wisdom, the more we can laugh at ourselves and at any difficult experience. It is often said that we must be wary of people that never or rarely laugh.

Laughter broadens our perspective, keeps us healthy and helps us overcome unbearable situations.

Laughter is the first step towards liberation. We start by laughing. We laugh so we unchain ourselves.

A smile is a treasure. The habit of smiling give us a facelift. Laugh often and your face will be shaped with a look of joy that will attract smiles and joy from others.

Be surrounded by people that make you laugh so often and out so loud that you forget your sufferings and reach more and more joy.

The smile you send always comes back to you.

Practice

This is the week to smile!!!

When you get up in the morning, you go to the bathroom mirror, and smile continuously for about twenty seconds, do this also before bedtime. During this week your goal is to make three people laugh per day, to find stories to tell, a joke to make or your formula that works to amuse your friends. Then in the evening, mark on your notebook the names of the people you made laugh.

Throughout this week, select TV programs, watch videos or go to the movies to see comedies, reading texts that make you laugh for sure.

"The most wasted of all days is the one when we did not laugh at all."

Sébastien-Roch Nicolas CHAMFORT

"When you rise in the morning give thanks for the light,
for your life, for your strength. Give thanks for the food
and for the joy of living. If you see no reason to give thanks,
the fault lies in yourself!"

TECUMSEH, Shawnee Chief

The expression "**THANK YOU**" emits a very powerful energy; it is the activator that allows us to receive everything in abundance. When we say "thank you" we send a very positive vibe with a feeling of having already received that immediately eliminates negativity. When we receive, what is happening? We feel good, we are happy. So the more we thank, the more we send the information and the message we already received, the more we receive again and again, it is as simple as that. It is setting up an automatic condition of *giving and receiving* in life.

Be grateful: thankfulness for every experience, every person in every moment, produces very quickly a positive change in life. Experience gratitude for all situations, even those that might seem negative. These are often the ones that make us evolve more. While being aware of this, thank life in all its forms, at every second, and it will give you back life situations in which you have the pleasure of giving thanks; that is the power of "thank you".

Practice

Divide a page along its width in your notebook. Every evening mark the three situations and the three people met during the day that you can say thank you to. There may of course be more depending on your choice and according to the progress of the attraction, but record at least six.

This exercise will help you learn to focus your attention on gratitude and the constructive elements of the joy of living and increase all the experiences in which we can say thank you, i.e. when we receive. It is good to engage in this practice just before bedtime, which allows to focus on the positive, to enjoy the best to finish the day, to cause pleasant dreams and get asleep peacefully.

"If, during your whole life, the only prayer you said was "Thank you," that would be sufficient."

ECKART TOLLE

"I have decided to be happy,
because it is good for health."

VOLTAIRE

This famous quote is part one of the most fundamental quote to insure our wellbeing and happiness, but often seems challenging to apply.

An unhealthy body produces an unhealthy mind and an unhealthy mind produces an unhealthy body.

Being happy or unhappy depends mainly on our perception of the situation, our ability to accept what we have or do not have; it is only a partial view of things and not a real observation of our situation.

When we are happy we emit emotions according to this state of mind. Our brain being capable of producing wellness hormones immediately spreads throughout the body, through the blood and lymph circulations, molecules that are good for health.

The opposite can occur: when we are unhappy we are focused on negative emotions that disrupt metabolism, affect our body and our health. We are therefore at any moment, facing this alternative:

- either *feel good,* which attracts positive life experiences and people that have this same energy;
- or *feel bad,* which lets in our lives the same experiences related to these negative energies.

Hurrah for life, when we are not dead! Simple, is it not?

Practice

One of the keys to feel good is to be aware of the specific emotions that make us feel good or not.

Getting up in the morning, read out loud this quote from Marcus Aurelius:

"When you arise in the morning, think of what a precious privilege it is to be alive - to breathe, to think, to enjoy, to love."

You can rephrase it this way:

"When I arise in the morning, I think of what a precious privilege it is to be alive - to breathe, to think, to enjoy, to love."

Then scroll through the list of positive and negative emotions following on the next pages; the goal is to know and be aware of them, because remember that whenever you experience these emotions, you are going to attract, in the following hours and days, the same experiences related to these emotions as well as to release in your body positive and negative hormones that impact your health. When you go to bed at night read only positive emotions, being aware of your every day progress.

"Like everyone else, I wanted everything; I sometimes obtained something, never everything.
Happiness has sometimes entered the desert in the absence of things; it sometimes snuck into clutter of too many things possessed. When it arrives, I know now that we should not ask it where it comes from, or who sends it; just be able to welcome it."

ALBERT JACQUARD

Cause negative emotion:

✓ to worry without reason;

✓ fear of losing self-control;

✓ targeted fears, phobias;

✓ panic, terror;

✓ jealousy and envy;

✓ difficulties to adapt to change;

✓ difficulty staying alone;

✓ impatience;

✓ doubt about one's judgment and decisions;

✓ dejection;

✓ resignation and abandonment;

✓ fatigue and weariness;

✓ intolerance, criticism;

✓ selfishness, possessiveness, demandingness;

✓ inflexibility, striving for perfection;

✓ enthusiasm to excess, willingness to impose one's beliefs;

✓ domination, tyranny;

✓ boredom, fed up, disgust.

Cause positive emotion:

✓ to accept one's qualities and flaws;
✓ self-confidence and feeling of security;
✓ tolerance;
✓ to give with wisdom and discernment;
✓ to reconnect with oneself;
✓ acceptance of lived experiences;
✓ dynamic, aware, enthusiastic;
✓ humor, taking responsibility, ambition;
✓ effectiveness and letting go;
✓ confidence and perseverance;
✓ faith and hope;
✓ altruism and listening skills;
✓ generosity and understanding;
✓ to restart, liveliness;
✓ tolerant, relaxed;
✓ capable, determined;
✓ self-assurance, peacefulness;
✓ stability, inner peace;
✓ regained energy;
✓ great courage;
✓ joy of living, flexible mind;
✓ light, emotion control;
✓ respect of others;
✓ calm mind;
✓ talent, ambition, purpose;
✓ gifts;
✓ pleasures;
✓ smiles;
✓ taking flight;
✓ victory;
✓ success.

> "When a wise man points at the Moon
> the fool examines the finger."
>
> CONFUCIUS

It is creativity that generates wealth and not the opposite. Discovering is seeing the same thing as everyone else and thinking differently.

It is precisely when we do not have wealth anymore that we create to have it back, for a renewal. An insecure and discomfort zone is often more beneficial because it allows us to break our habits and learn how to do better and see differently.

Adversity always offers more strength than harm because it prevents stagnation. It is always a starting point and not an end.

Learn to see everything and every situation in a new light is the key to generating wealth and discover what has not been discovered yet. With an open mind we see beyond what we perceived in front of us, in the immediate future. Let go the blinders and desert platitudes. To think otherwise is first to open one's mind to see further, much further...

Practice

Before learning how to think and see things differently, it is essential not to be short-sighted.

To start programming this new vision in your brain, make it a habit to look up for the most distant element that your eye can see (in a room pay attention to the most distant object, outside pay attention to what you can see as far away as possible in the landscape.)

This exercise is very simple and will quickly develop in you the spirit of discovery seeing further.

This week pay attention to that as often as possible.

"Who, being loved, is poor?"

OSCAR WILDE

Be with your friends for what they are and not for what they might bring you; your relationships will then be even richer and more plentiful.

Each person that comes to you brings you a message; pay attention to it. Surround yourself with those that bring out the best in you. Humans need real contacts to survive and prosper. Communicate regularly with your family, friends, send messages saying: "hello I'm thinking of you!".
Do not miss the opportunity to hug and kiss our loved ones, not just those who live with you. Train yourself to feel and rejoice of hearts that meet, of friends, of office colleagues, etc. Saying "I love you" is beneficial to both the giver and the receiver.
The distance may be physically large but souls are still close. Souls can love each other without there minds being aware of it. This is why, often when the spirits rest at night, the souls of those who love each other are communicating and communing with each other.

When you look at the stars, think that each star is one of your bright and magical thoughts, and that you send them to all those who crossed your path. There are so many beautiful people on our lifepath, that if we look carefully, we only see that: a lot of gratitude...

Practice

Every day, take at least one new person in your arms and tell this person "I love you or I adore you." Think it sincerely (if you feel embarrassed to do, tell this person that it is in the context of an exercise and offer this person to do the same). This exercise will bring you and give your audience a powerful recognition of love. If this week you do not have enough opportunity to meet people for this exercise, write messages to a different person each day saying, I think of you or I love you.

Do not forget to transcribe the names of every person on your notebook.

"Think, in a word, that it is to make happy
your fellows, to heal, to help,
and to love them that nature puts you in their midst,
and not to judge, punish
and especially not to lock them in."

MARQUIS de SADE

> "Forgiveness is washing one's brushes to get back
> to paint an even more beautiful painting."
>
> ALLAN D. LEBKOY

The weakest retaliate, the strongest forgive and the happiest forget.

What is your choice?
When we forgive we do not change the past, but we for sure change the future. It is only by forgiving that miracles happen. The healing of body and mind can only take place once we have forgiven.
Life is too short to waste time hating someone. Free yourself from negative ties of the past with those that have offended you or hurt you, and those you have hurt or offended. Do not keep regret or remorse in you. Otherwise it will prevent you from moving on in the life you want to have.
As long as that part of yourself is not cleaned, all the old patterns will be engraved and stuck in your body. They materialize in unconscious negative energies and attract to you the same experiences related to similar sufferings.

Everything must be forgivable and forgivable does not mean acceptable. To avoid being rigid and intolerant, put your finger on the underside of your wrist to feel your heart pulse. It is a way to remember that we have a heart that beats just like the people we are going to forgive.
To detach ourselves from a part of our past to help ourselves forgive does not mean to forget it.

The memories and experiences inevitably remain, but they only represent part of what you are at this moment. It is in this that you have the choice to forgive and focus all your energy to build the future instead of fighting against the past.

Practice

During this week you will free yourself from all ties that block your progress. Take time each day to write on a sheet of paper (but not in your notebook) all situations in your life when you hurt someone, even unconsciously or unintentionally and those in which it is you that have been bruised. Feel the emotions that those memories remind you. Then, store the paper in a small box. On Sunday, light a candle. Tear the paper, strongly, into small pieces, pronouncing the formula: we are now collectively healed and forgiven, healed and forgiven, healed and forgiven...
Then burn the pieces of paper and throw the ashes into the toilets or a river saying now all ties and negative psychic connections are definitely cut and surrounded by a beautiful light enveloping everyone of us.

"If there is one unforgivable thing, it is not to forgive."

ROMAIN GARY

"When you do something,
know that you will have against you those who would like to do
the same thing, those who wanted to do the opposite
and the vast majority of those who did not want to do anything."

CONFUCIUS

At any action opposes a reaction of equal strength. There is only one step between being able to and not being able to.
This step can totally change your destiny.

When you make a decision, you emit a very important message around you.
And only if the decision is followed by action in the following hours will it manifest its full power, even beyond what you could imagine.
Eliminating the time between an idea and its implementation will make your dreams come true.
Do not wait. Start immediately. When we are waiting it is because we hesitate, that there are doubts and therefore resistance that hinder us.

And this is the message that we send to our subconscious that will keep things on hold, even if we have made an important decision.
Without the application of the corresponding action, it is as if we were canceling any impulse at the very moment of starting.

Practice

This week's exercise will be to implement the decisions that will make life changes you desire possible.

Make a list of everything you want to change or improve in your life.

For example losing weight. If you take the decision to lose weight, engage immediate action in the next few hours, to get the desired result. It may be, for example, to eat differently, to do sports, buy a book on nutrition, take an appointment with a coach, etc.

Then, take the habit during this week and the following ones, each time you get an idea or you take a decision, to have your intention quickly followed by an action.

This will cause a movement of energy that will make things progress, even if later you change your mind.

You will have at least started a movement instead of your decision to stay still in the state of a thought that will perhaps never occur.

"You have to play to get serious…"

ARISTOTLE

Playing with life, creating the distance between life and death, and between health and illness is to keep the eternity of youthful mind and this will affect our whole life.

Life is a great game! Find the way to create the rules that will always allow you to win. Life is an adventure, a stage where everyone has a role to play, and a role that is constantly evolving.

Do you know what yours is?
Your role to play is the one with you as the author and actor, the one you are having fun with, where you love what you do and what you are.
And most importantly, you can change it when you want to get a better role.

To play with life is not to take it seriously, it is to learn how not to worry. When we play, we may be afraid of losing but not of dying, so by playing we move away from death and we stimulate life!
A child plays with lightness without worrying about life; an adult sometimes cannot even remember the last time he played.

Practice

This week is the week when you relax through playing.
There are of course many ways to play: with one's children, a pet or a group. And there are lots of games: games of skills and chance, questions and answers, board games... etc. To make things easier, the game this week will be the same for everyone.
But nothing prevents you to integrate all the human beings that share your life.
Ten minutes a day (preferably in the evening), you will do your best clown, disguise yourself with a hat, a little makeup, a head scarf may do the trick, be creative changing every day. Position yourself in front of a mirror then put your favorite music, which always makes you into a good mood. And dance, dance, dance...
It is possible that you are so relaxed by this little exercise that you might want to repeat beyond a week. Of course, you can repeat it as long as you want.

> "It is not the fear of madness which will force us
> to drop the flag of imagination."
>
> ANDRÉ BRETON

Your mind is like a painter's canvas.
What you represent on the canvas of your mind is what you will paint in your life. The power of the word Imagine is magical...
It is the source of all creation. Dreaming of something is the first step towards realization. Your imagination has no boundaries...
Close your eyes for a moment and pronounce slowly:

Imagine...

Imagine everything you want to have, be or do... Imagine life as you want to see it. The impossible becomes possible when we imagine. When space is left between our tens of thousands of daily thoughts (50,000 on average) to allow room for the creation of our imagination, we are able to achieve what we visualized and felt deep inside of us.
Whatever the size of your vision, it will be equivalent to the size of your accomplishments.

Think big is living big.

Practice

You become what you think about most often, so you become what you imagine most often and what you see most often. How do you imagine every part of your life in terms of: health, love and money?

The exercise this week is to decorate one or more spaces, at your workplace or at home, with photos that make you dream, about all the themes of life.

Choose what you think is the best in your areas of interest. Each photo must emit a vibration of dream.

Use your imagination and renovate every corner of your life that does not inspire feelings of happiness.

Remember that if you see negative pictures or movies you will attract negative in your life; on the opposite if you pay attention most often to positive images, situations or movies, your life will open to the positive, to peace and well-being.

"Enjoy and give joy, without harming yourself or anyone else:
here lies, I think, all the morality."

SÉBASTIEN-ROCH NICOLAS CHAMFORT

Enjoy what the five senses offer you, unexpected situations, what the eye catches, scents, touch, encounters, we must first exist to learn how to live. Light is everywhere, even in the dark, it is just a matter of wanting to see it and then we see it.

The way we look at things brings to us **the just reward.**

If you look at things - and therefore life - with contempt and hatred, you will receive only hatred and contempt. Look at things with appreciation, seeking to always notice the positive side of situations and people. Persisting to seek the good in every person you meet brings out the good side of people and opens the door anywhere and any situation.

Admire the best in yourself and in those around you. Learn to see the beauty and goodness in everything, in every experience, every person and at every moment; as a child, who observes without judging.

Learn to see the best in others, learn to see in their heart and soul, and in their eyes! First do not stop at what your eyes see and what your ears hear, then just try to feel with your heart what is best in others.

Practice

This week, you are going to acquire new eyes and a new perspective.

Make it a habit every day to watch the people around you with your heart, your feeling, without judgment, just observe.

Then, in each person and each situation look for the positive side, there is always one.

For example, direct your benevolent look on a person you know, who is authoritarian and unsympathetic, and imagine this person playing with his/her children with great joy or cherishing a loved one, caressing his/her favorite pet, enjoying with delight a dessert that he/she loves, you can imagine what makes yourself happy without limits and transfer it to the person you have chosen.

Thinking this way you will change the vibe facing this person and provoke a positive energy return. Note in the evening emotions felt about these experiences.

You find that the result is so powerful that you will never be able to see people differently thereafter, or do without this healthy exercise.

"Those who do not believe in magic
will never find some."

Roald DAHL

Anything your mind can believe, it can achieve.

To believe in something, a dream in you, is the fundamental point for any beginning.
If you do not believe, life cannot be possible…
It is often difficult to believe because the mind needs to see in order to believe, but in reality the process is the opposite, **it is only if you believe that you see.**
Remember well this statement: here in lies all the difference. When you really believe, nothing can destroy this belief and the idea driven by that belief will inevitably *materialize*. Often we do not want to believe because we do not have the vision of how things will occur.
Therefore to believe is first of all to trust. It is the faith in the manifestation of any idea that our mind has tirelessly forged with intensity.

The unrelenting focus with all our faith leads to the materialization and allows what was originally only in the field of thought to take form.
This is the whole meaning of this dictum that says "faith can move mountains". *Not only can it move mountains, but the belief in the power of your mind can create a new landscape, where it is nice to live.*
This dream that we carry within us, if we think of it often enough, will sooner or later come true.

To believe and achieve absolute efficiency, it is imperative to remove every doubt, eradicate any resistance.

Doubt annihilates our energy, seizes up our life force and affects our core belief by suggesting negative thoughts that limit our field of action.

Go beyond your need to see before believing.

If you believe in it, then you will see it.

All things are possible to the one who believes.

The only belief that counts, is the one that belongs to the deepset past of us and that we can change at any time when our truth evolves.

The magic of life is to believe that the best is still to come...

"Faith is taking the first step even when you cannot see the whole staircase."

MARTIN LUTHER KING

Practice

This practical application increases the belief that whatever you imagine and think very intensely will sooner or later happen.

Every morning write a list of small things of everyday life that you would like to have. Once this is done, think of all the aspects that please you imagining them **already** achieved.

Use the magic words of gratitude: thank you, thank you, thank you for this wonderful lunch I had with... which brought me a lot of pleasure (for example).

Do it for all your activities of the day and also for other unplanned things you want.

Then in the evening reread your list and you will see the number of things that happened, even beyond your expectations.

This will increase your faith and belief that anything you imagine intensely you will get.

As explained at the beginning of the book do not believe what you read, but trust what you are going to practice. By practising this exercise and observing the results, this belief will become yours and nothing can make you think otherwise.

LET US LOOK BACK AT THE JOURNEY MADE

You have discovered during the first three months the importance to give to your dream and the first means to change your life and your perception of the world. You practice regularly and enjoy the proposed exercises as you can already see the power of "thank you", forgiveness and the relationship with those you love. You have realized that the method is right and begins to bear fruit. In order to transform our life and make it more beautiful we just need to change our habits and our relationship to events. You understand the power of this way of life because it is not a new theory, but concrete actions, daily and renewed practices. Remember that the important thing is not what you read, but what you are experiencing. It is not the thought but the practice that transforms life. You understand that you can use or repeat such an exercise more frequently, because it touches you inside your heart. However, you must carry on learning on the same path; because this is how the method show its effectiveness. In the next few weeks, you are going to adopt the right attitude, experience the power of giving, strengthen your self-confidence and finally approach life with joy and hope. You will see with pleasure that if life is a serious thing, there is no point to be too serious yourself.

Make sure to always have your notebook with you in which you will write down the laws that are most important for you and above all the changes you notice in you and dates of your comments and your successes in order to follow the progress made on the path you have chosen to enrich your life.

Week 13 - Choose the right attitude!

> "Nothing can stop the man with the right mental attitude from achieving his goal; nothing on earth can help the man with the wrong mental attitude."
>
> THOMAS JEFFERSON

Take the attitude of the person you want to be and you will become like this person.

You want to be successful in your business: take the attitude of those that have already succeeded.

Your attitude should then be visible as much as possible in this way of being.

You want to live in happiness and love with the man or woman of your life: have the attitude of the joy that this desired union provides. This attitude displays "class", the wisdom to choose poise when facing any situation. It is the expression of your inner vibration that affects your appearance for all situations.

Choose the right attitude. Choose only the thoughts that put you a in a good mood, do not accept the others! It is only by changing your attitude that you determine your altitude.

Within seconds you can change your attitude; with these few seconds you change your day.

Practice

This week, you only have to think about your high attitude. The one that makes you feel powerful, strong and happy! The physical aspect will help you for this exercise.

When you walk, imagine that you have springs under your feet, as if you rebound at every step, try walking like that and you see the effect it has on the brain and affects your attitude.

Without bragging, with simplicity, just take the attitude of someone powerful, a samurai, a knight, an actor or actress you admire, according to the image that you have of someone from whom emanates strength, elegance and vitality.

Pulling your shoulders back as much as possible without arching or overly emphasizing the chest, has a very important effect to help you feel better.

On the contrary, when we do not feel well and we fall back on ourselves, we are more saggy and our breathing is less easy.

Your attitude is right when your face is relaxed; you smile. Ask yourself the question: how is my face at the moment? What can you immediately do to change this?

✓ Learn to walk tall, bounce and carry your shoulders back.

✓ Relax your face and keep a smile as often as possible and always have an open and frank expression as if you are about to change the world or make happy the people you walk by.

✓ Whenever you enter a place, you meet a person, bring happiness to tell yourself: what is my desire for this situation?

Think about the vibration it emits in you and the satisfaction of having already achieved what you want.

Feel like a prince, strong, powerful, happy, who is warmly welcomed, and gets everything he wants!

> "When the mind says: "Give up",
> hope whispers: "Try once again" ".
>
> Mongolian Proverb

As long as there is hope there is life... Only hope brings us forward. When there is life, there is movement.

The cycles are constantly changing, nothing is ever static, even if things seem slow sometimes.

However the situation is not stagnant, so there is hope. Giving up kills **any** chance of hope and success. Do not give up, keep on planting and watering the seeds that germinate when the ground is conducive to harvest.

You might see nothing happen during a season; this is no reason to cut the tree you planted and has still not produced anything, it is there. Keep on taking care of it, it will eventually produce what you expect.

Hope is to have faith, believe again and again, always believe that everything will be fine, that things are as they should be and in the end everything will be perfect.

To hope is to trust life; it is often at the last minute when we no longer believe, in cases of the great despair that the miracle arises spontaneously.

But for this miracle to occur, one must believe in it, believe, always hoping for the best in every situation, that things will always eventually improve to our advantage.

Hope is what leads us to our accomplishment.

Practice

This is the week of great hopes.

What can help maintaining hope is to see that things are not stopped, that they are moving forward, even if slowly.

Every little successful step made in this direction is a step towards your goal. These successes are there to encourage you and let you hope for the best.

The exercise is to write every day of this week before bedtime, in your little notebook, *all the small successes you have had* during the day that bring you closer to your goal and allow you to increase in faith and hope.

This exercise that may seem easy to you will make you focus on one aspect of positive thinking; the hope for the best that you can have in any situation and thus gradually creating this reality.

> "It is not how much we give
> but how much love we put into giving."
>
> MOTHER TERESA

Give the best you can give with the best intention.

A little, a lot, passionately, madly... Give your smile. Let it shine around you. Give your courage.

Let it support the others. Give your enthusiasm, your trust and your love.

The smallest things for you can seem huge to someone else.

Whenever you give, you enrich a part of the soul of another person and you feel really good.

Happiness implies giving freely to others.

Life is a constant exchange of energy.

We have inside of us huge treasures that we can share around us.

We can offer at least our time to help anyone in need.

It is only in giving that we receive.

Whenever we give we get it back five times in return, even if the return does not seem always instant or if it takes a different form. If you feel that you do not get enough, so give more, give without counting, expectation of return, fear of missing, just give and you will receive quickly.

One of the most important laws of the universe is **the law of compensation.**

Everything is always right.

You reap everything you sow; it cannot be otherwise.

If you give to others, others will give to you, if you take advantage of others and do not give to them, others will take advantage of you so you will get very little.

Who has given should never remember that he has.

Anyone who knows how to give more than he thinks he has is actually much richer than the one who thinks he owns and does not know how to give. *Who has received should never forget that he has.*

The more we share the more we own.

Practice

This week you will focus your attention on the law of Giving. Think all day about giving, you have within you the abundance of all things and you can share without counting. Take this habit of giving to everyone you meet.

A compliment, a smile, a good deed, money, time, support, prayer, affection, attention...

You always have something to give the other does not have. When you give it must be natural, so it is not useful to remember it.

But this week, just for the sake of the exercise, write on your notebook or on a separate page, each time you gave something.

At least you will have given ten times a day. Then reread this list before you go to sleep. This practice causes a feeling of magnificent well-being and a feeling of being richer inside.

Giving activates inside us a feeling of enormous joy, causes a new dimension of our being. Giving whenever we can results in us being able to give more and to receive more, and thus to continue to give more.

This is the energy flow of life which leads to our receiving more, the more we give.

If we stop giving, we do not receive anymore.

"Prayer is not just asking;
it is a longing of the soul."

MAHATMA GANDHI

Prayer is the most important connection that our mind emits to obtain our requests. No need for a religion, or specific ritual to pray, just the feeling that comes from the heart, what you want most.

Prayer is primarily a request to the Universe, God, the source, whatever your religion is. Repeated prayers very often have the power to materialize. To think for a few minutes without interruption creates a magical wave that has already manifested itself in the reality of one's mind.

To practice on a regular basis causes a change that will manifest sooner or later in your physical reality.

For the emission of a prayer to work it must be a positive thought, like an affirmation.

It is critical to understand that it gives joy and wellbeing thinking about it.

The mood at the time of the prayer is crucial for the realization of the request. Often people pray thinking only about a lack to fill.

They pray for not being sick instead of praying for being healthy. To pray is to believe that we have already received.

The physical manifestation in present reality comes when we no longer hold on and are being attached to our prayer, when we are able to let go and place ourselves in the hands of superior forces of destiny and life.

Practice

This week you are going to work on your ability to connect in prayer to obtain your requests.

Connect above (whatever your belief is).

Ask, pray, and then, above all, let it happen. Do not be impatient with the result, let it happen and let go...

Make a habit of asking fifty times a day, feeling joy and gratitude to have already obtained what you ask for.

Make simple requests and prayers.

For example: thank you, thank you, thank you for this parking space one step away from my office. Thank you, thank you, thank you to be well guided in this store to find the product I want.

It is not about looking for the extraordinary, but making the ordinary exceptional.

Take advantage of the power of prayer to give ten percent of what you get (tithing). This is a tiny fraction of gifts received to thank life and thank others for all the benefits granted.

Every day, address a prayer for several people.

For example:

"Thank you, thank you, thank you for the good recovery of X... bringing him a maximum of smiles in his life."

By exercising your prayers for a week, you will then understand the power of prayer and you will not be able to function without it.

> "Logic will take you from point A to point B,
> imagination will take you everywhere."
>
> ALBERT EINSTEIN

People are so afraid to dare to live what they desire that they remain cloistered in their comfort zones, their trust circle with limited outlook.

If you were going to die in seven days, what would you do during this last week? Perhaps you would enjoy life to its maximum, as you have never done before... Maybe you would go to meet your beloved, to live your passion without fear and limit...

Maybe you would spend and enjoy all your money without thinking about tomorrow... And the list goes on.

Above all you would finally dare to do what you have never dared to do when you thought you had a lifetime ahead of you. Make yours this famous quote that says: *"If you do what you have always done, you will get what you always got. If you want things to change you must first change the things you usually do."*

Meditate on this commandment which is really the basis of everything. Dare to do things differently, dare to change your social environment, where you hang out, etc.

Take risks; get out of your comfort zone.

By remaining in your world and in your habits, not daring to change, things change only very slowly or not at all.

Fire up your passions and live them!

Be prepared to change your habits if you want to change your future.

Dare to think differently to live the life you really want to live.

Dare to do things you have never done and will you get things that you have never dared to imagine having.

Practice

Make a list of several things you do not dare doing.

These can be simple things, such as for example for a shy person to ask the time to someone in the street.

Be honest with yourself and do it as a game, have fun.

From this list, begin this week to commit yourself to the topics you have chosen, starting with the one you think is easier and ending with the most difficult one that you will have achieved at the end of the week.

This exercise is absolutely magical, it is going to help your mind adapt to circumstances and get you out of your protective cocoon; to overcome your fears, to go beyond your limits, to expand your thinking and very quickly give you the power to change things in your life.

"A human being has this need to control everything;
so afraid he is to lose control.
The more we hold on to things, to people,
the more we lose them; the more we trust,
the more we get, it is really so simple."

When you try to control everything, you do not enjoy any moment. Yet it is at this moment when you do not intend to lose control that you must let go.

Control is never in the present moment, never in the action of the here and now, but rather in the fear of the future or the suffering of the past.

Controlling is always in the spirit and the mind, letting go is in the heart.

Go to the center of yourself, the very essence of your being.

Let the situation flow, let it go, let it breathe until the moment when you have no more control over events; and it is when they start to be beyond control that they begin to materialize...

As soon as you accept, you release what you had refused and held imprisoned inside you.

Your mind becomes free, naturally serene, as unstirred water is clear by nature.

Humanity produces its own fears by thinking about its demons. There is still time and it is always possible to change our way of building just by changing our way of thinking. There are only two camps, either be in love, or in fear.

Practice

For this week's exercise, remember this: it is always the fear of losing that prevents us of letting go.

Whenever you are unable to let go, ask yourself the question sincerely: what am I afraid of losing?

Give it up, drop it and tell yourself that if you have lost something, it is better for you, because something better will come to you soon.

If you fear losing your job, in most cases it is pointless to worry about it excessively, but it is best to engage all your strength and all your attention in the search for a more suitable activity while respecting the laws already experienced, to make every effort to transform things according to the law of attraction.

If you are worried that your partner will leave you, say to yourself that it is better that he/her leaves, and imagine another person later in your life that will give you more satisfaction.

For this to work, you have to really sincerely think it. In doing so, you will release energy blocks and you will be amazed at the results.

It is quite possible, if this is the fairest solution that your spouse may come back to you running.

Whenever you think you will lose, immediately think what positive gain you will get in return.

"You must learn to be still in the midst of the activity
and to be vibrantly alive in repose."

Mahatma GANDHI

We are all made up of atoms and energy.
One of the only things that differentiates us is our frequency.
This is one of the most important secrets to how we draw all things to us.

The higher your vibration, so your frequency, the more you will attract similar high frequencies.
To raise one's frequency is above all to be aware of everything that brings it down.

First, anything that creates a negative thought in you inevitably drops your vibrational level.
Negative thinking is usually identified by a situation we do not want, or not anymore, and of course by negative surroundings.

A negative vibration essentially comes from the mind, of reminders of past sufferings or of fears of the future, and on the contrary a positive vibration comes from deep inside you, from the feeling of your heart at this present moment.

Practice

This week, you should think about this mantra at least a hundred times a day:

My frequency is high now!

Whisper it at least a hundred times a day, and it will effectively increase your vibrational frequency and attract positive situations.

While whispering the phrase, put your attention primarily on what is beautiful, useful and enjoyable.

Ignore negative thoughts and influences and all places that would be in contradiction.

You will see in just a few days what will happen around you by focusing your mind on a high vibration.

> "The miracle of love is not to love a man
> or a woman: it is to love yourself just enough to be
> able to truly love another person."
>
> ROGER FOURNIER

Being in the peace of one's heart, it is the only thing that matters...
Love is to love - Being happy is to love yourself and love others!

The worst prison is the one of a closed heart; open your heart to the rhythm of each beat, love tirelessly, love again and again, the power of love exceeds the fear of not loving and not being loved.

Those who do not like us, in general do not like themselves.
For love, it is therefore necessary to vibrate at the same frequency with the same understanding of things; otherwise it is just an illusion.
It is by loving that we are loved and that is sharing our heart that we receive... Do you live your love as you would like? Do you receive? Do you give? Love is the greatest force in the universe. When you give, you receive back. Love opens hearts and makes our perception of the world better and more positive, exciting and motivating.

Love gives you wings, leads to action; while often disease comes from a lack of self-love.
Be close only to those that are close to you for real...
Let others live their close horizon away from you; take time with those who are trully close and you will save a lot of time.

Sooner or later life brings the people destined to meet who vibrate together at the same frequency. Visualizing that the perfect person for you, the one for you, comes at the right moment, allows that dream to come true.

To love a woman or a man can change the world, our world and her/his world.
In order to love we must learn to look beyond our world, limits and habits; take interest in the world of the other.
The egocentric does not know what to love is, he/she cannot love and suffers, because his/her requirement can never reach the perfection sought.
To love is to give up control of the mind for the benefit of the perfection of love.
Be surrounded only by people that want to love without expectations, to madness, with passion... just simply live love.

Because a human being is biologically made to love, it is this energy that nourishes our 10 billion cells and allows the regeneration of new ones and good health.

The secret of a long life in good health;

IS TO LOVE!!

Those who have not been burned at least once in love have not really lived life, but those who have lived it and that no longer believe in love, do not understand life; what matters most in our existence, is love, the rest we do not care, it is the only belief that should be indestructible.

Practice

This week here is a very simple exercise with the choice of words below.

They will give you a positive vibration.

Remember, every word emits a vibration, a frequency that modulates gradually your unconscious mind.

Read it every morning thinking about the smile of a child, a loved one, the joy of humanity, or a tangible friend...

WARNING!

ABUSE OF LOVE IS NEVER DANGEROUS FOR HEALTH!

COMPANION, WELLBEING, PLEASURE, GAIETY, IN LOVE, REJOICE YOURSELF, ENJOY, HAVE FUN, LIVE, BREATHE, BE GOOD TO YOURSELF, GIVE YOURSELF A GOOD LIFE, HAPPINESS, HEALTHY, SERENITY, DREAMY, QUIET SAFETY COMFORT, TRANQUILITY, GOOD, WELL, PLEASANT, HARMONY, GLEE, ZEN COOL, FULLNESS, LUXURY, CALM, PLEASURE, JOY, ENCHANTMENT, DELIGHTS, EASE, GLEE, JUBILATION, TO SAVOR, EXULTATION, ARDOR, PEACEFULL, CARESSES, IN PEACE, ABUNDANCE, MARVELOUS, EXCELLENCE BEAUTY JOY, HAPPY, EASY POSITIVE MUSIC, REWARDING, FRUITFUL, USEFUL, ADVANTAGES, TO SAVOR, ENTHUSIASM, APPRECIATE, RESPECT, TASTE, ORGASM, FRAGRANCE, GENTLENESS, WRIGGLE, CARING, SOFT, FREE, TENDER, COMFORTABLE FRESHNESS, CUDDLY, DELICACY, TO EXULT, FRIENDSHIP, LOVE, FERVOR, POWERFUL REASSURING, LAUGH, SOOTHING, SOLID STABILITY, HUMAN, ALIVE, KISSES, STRETCHING, GENEROUS...

CONSIDERATE, TENDERNESS, PASSION, JUBILATION, FELICITY, CARING, EXHILARATION, FAVORABLE, GRACIOUS, MATERNAL, IN LOVE, REST, COURTESY, WELCOMING, MOMENTUM, EXULT, WONDER, GIVING, OFFERING, ENTHUSIASM, GENEROSITY, GRACIOUSLY, UNCTUOUS, FREE, SMILE, PLEASURE, KINDLY, CHARMING, ENCHANTING, SEDUCTIVE, BENEFICIAL, CAJOLING, PAMPERING, COCOONING, CUDDLING, GROOMING, CODDLING, CARESSING, CHERISHING, FILLING, CRADLING, LOOK AFTER BABIES, TREASURING, AFFECTIONATE, ASSIST, SUPPORT, HELP OUT, WARRANTY, DELICACY...

LOVE, LOVE, LOVE...

> "The humble man is not affected by praise
> or insults of others.
> His self-esteem is only coming from himself."
>
> (ANONYMOUS)

Others are undermining my self-confidence and self-esteem; yet no one should assume such power over me. Confidence must come from within, from our own experience, our own judgment and our own beliefs; otherwise any event will make it wobble.

The one who desperately seeks attention of others has not yet found his true self. He is not aware of his true value. Without self-esteem he depends on the opinion of others. He is dependent on their praise, because without their appreciation he feels unworthy.

Self-confidence is the first step towards your success.
Listening to your inner voice, trusting it, giving it all powers, is ensuring your true personal development.
To have self-confidence is also to trust others and move forward all together.

Practice

It often takes a lifetime to learn to have confidence, but in only one week we can already make a big difference.

The problem of lack of self-confidence is that we have focused our attention too much on our failures and our weaknesses instead of paying attention to our advantages and strengths.

This week you are sending your resume to the Universe.

Make a list of your ten most outstanding points, of your assets, of what you like to do often, of your know-hows, skills, hobbies, expertise, etc.

Read this list in the morning and evening, feel what it brings to you to know all that you are worth, it will have a beneficial effect, will make you stronger and in the same way, make your weak points insignificant.

Remember! A weak point is never transformed into a strong point, but by giving it attention you reduce your self-confidence.

By focusing as often as possible your attention on your strengths, you will increase your confidence in general; and you weaknesses will be almost invisible so overshadowed are they by your strengths.

"Knowledge speaks,
but wisdom listens."

JIMI HENDRIX

Listening is to know how to listen to everything we do not want to hear yet.
God gave us two ears and one mouth, use them proportionally; listen twice as much as you talk.
Silence your mind, let the ones that always have something to say speak, let them have the last word. The most talkative are not the ones with the most interesting things to say.

True knowledge and wisdom is knowing to clear your mind when necessary, knowing when to shut up and communicating precisely at the right time.
Silent knowledge comes when you know how to listen to the silence.
Listen to other points of view without being distracted.
It is by listening that we learn best.

Life sends us messages at every moment, to learn to listen to them, is to know how to surrender. Letting go of critical thinking and control allows us to empty our mind leaving room for receiving messages.

Practice

This week you will listen to everything you have not been able to hear yet.

Pay attention to every conversation whether you shut up and listen to your partner without interruption, mark a moment of silence when he has finished speaking.

Then speaking with moderation and accuracy will only increase the quality and strength of your words.

Pay attention all week being a good listener, to everything that you can listen to in your environment.

Listening has the immense advantage of disconnecting you from your mind and bringing you back into the present moment which is the instant that gives you your true power.

> "People that do not laugh at all
> are not serious people."
>
> ALPHONSE ALLAIS

Have fun and dance with life, this will prevent you from taking yourself too seriously.

Those who take themselves too seriously in life are often the weakest are taking on a role, an appearance and a false personality; their inside is indeed empty and sad.

Those who are serious in life and do things seriously just do not take themselves seriously. An excess of seriousness is the expression of a trapped life filled with restrictions, preventing joy and laughter to emerge and spread. STOP TAKING YOURSELF SERIOUSLY: taking yourself seriously does not change anything, except making you a little bit more tense...

Every event that happens to us always seems at first more serious than it actually is; so wait a little bit to avoid to get upset... You will feel better later. Not taking oneself seriously improves mood and allows one to let go. The humor and derision, especially self-depreciating, are the best remedies to increase joy. Blessed are those who can laugh and be entertained by not taking themselves too seriously. Wisdom belongs to those who smile and laugh without restriction or limitation.

Not taking yourself seriously promotes laughter and humor.
Who knows how to laugh and smile, embrace's life and knows how to cultivate joy.

Do not take yourself seriously, but seriously have fun.

Practice

The exercise of this week is to integrate this chapter by heart by reading it slowly several times a day.

You always learn a lot by watching others; pay attention to those who take themselves too seriously and those who are relaxed with life while being serious in their activities.

Then come back each time on yourself at any time of day. And honestly answer the to following questions:

Am I taking myself seriously now?

Why do I adopt this attitude?

What am I afraid of?

And once you have found the answer, you can laugh at yourself, saying to yourself anyway we all eventually die, so what is the point in taking ourselves so seriously?

"Joy is a state of transcendence.
One is neither happy nor unhappy,
but utterly peaceful, quiet, in absolute equilibrium."

Osho DHAMMAPADA

To be in the joy of life consists in seeing the extraordinary in the ordinary at every moment. Nobody has the right to prevent you from being happy.

Joy is the ultimate step above happiness, joy just IS, as the sun gives us life and warms us.

Joy is connected to the path leading to the soul and is not related to a project, a person or an object that can be found somewhere outside of us.

Joy is immaterial: it is a concept that is foremost essential to learn and grow in order to achieve excellence in life.

Be **JOYFUL** as often as possible without trying to find a reason, fully accept who you are.

When you live in joy you naturally live in love.

Practice

Joy and ecstasy oppose any control and limitation structure.
When you are happy you are truly free.
It is then impossible to be controlled by anyone.
This is why power structures (religions, governments and institutions) that understood that well promote fear and not joy; because there is no way to manage or control someone that lives in joy.
The exercise this week is to assimilate well the notion of joy, which is the true path to self-realization.
This obviously will not be done in a week but gradually, progressively. But it is important to integrate as fast as possible the necessary tools to practice for better assimilation. Beyond the text of this chapter that you can often read, choose readings that open your heart, elevate your soul. Always choose what is full of life and joy.
A little exercise also very powerful to focus your attention as often as possible on a state of joy is to take a few minutes several times a day to remind you especially feel inside you, an experience, a relationship a gift that brought you this feeling of happiness.
While these moments are related to people or material aspects that should not be dependent on the fact of being in the joy, in this exercise you will first increase your vibration letting you approach joy a little bit more.

> "I know and I feel that to do good is the trueest happiness
> that a human heart can taste."
>
> Jean-Jacques ROUSSEAU

To see the bright side of your life, you must perceive the inside of people and things retaining what is best in them.

See only the good around you, even if appearances may seem unpleasant, your vision will have the power to change your reality. To have goodness in all situations and with every person makes you emit a power that emanates from your body and mind, which is perceived by others giving you the best protection against negative influences.

Someone that has goodness inside him and vibrates love cannot be affected by the shadow. There will always be beautiful days for those who have goodness in their heart. This simple attitude to be full of goodness will produce a snowball effect on one's surroundings.

When we do something good to someone, that person will unconsciously pass on the goodness to another and so on.

Observe how your friends deal with the people around them and like this you will know how they will treat you eventually.

Practice

The attraction and compensation law acts with goodness as with everything else.

However, the more you offer goodness at every occasion around you, the more everyone you meet will help you and guide you.

The exercise of this week that you can also continue thereafter is to brighten the day of people you approach with small simple gestures.

Be kind. Stay calm when stressed people pass by.

For example, at the checkout queue in a department store let someone with only a few items go in front of you, help someone that is lost, needs explanation or help people in any other situation where you can bring improvement, as often as you would like it to be done for you.

Give importance to the people you meet, take time for them; if they are people you do not know it will have even more importance for them.

> "It is not the abundance,
> but excellence which is wealth."
>
> Joseph JOUBERT

Abundance is everywhere on Earth, in water, in air, with the sun and especially in life which has never been as developed as today. It is the misuse of abundant resources by humanity that makes us believe its limits.

To receive in abundance, there is only one rule to apply: think big! Think without limits of space nor time. Drop the belief that things in your life may be limited.

Abundance in health is a happy state of mind promoting joy and well being at any time of the day. This is the only concern you should continuously have.
Real beauty of life, is when you love someone so strongly... that the abundance of love manifesting, attracts to us prosperity in other areas.

Abundance in money is to know that resources are unlimited, money is just a way to buy more time and comfort to satisfy one's desires.
To attract money in abundance one just needs to have desires and want to live them. Those who have abundance in their lives have decided to live their lives without limits and without restrictions.

Practice

Be in abundance at every moment. To attract abundance you have to live as if you already possess it.

Imagine having all the money you dream of having, the best relationships and exceptional health. What would be your attitude in this state of mind? If reading this question gives you doubts, it is that you have already put a stop to any possibility of abundance.

The secret of abundance is not to worry about lacking.

Be ready to let go to get more. Being in abundance is to give in abundance around us.

Your exercise this week is to give around you to experience this abundance. You will see after a week you receive more; because we get what we live and not the opposite. If you want abundance in health, be plentiful to yours by taking good care of yourself.

Also give health to others through your positive attitude, your advice or anything that might help someone to get better.

If you want abundance in love and better relationships, be loving and kind to others. If you want plenty of money, be generous with money, invite your friends, buy them gifts, spoil them, give and share without keeping records of what you have paid.

Six months already

You have now practiced for six months the exercises related to the fifty-two laws that have already begun to transform your life. It is important to take stock before continuing this daily practice which in reality is a reshaping of yourself and becomes your lifestyle.

You can rejoice in dealing with lightness but intensity with events and people around you. It is not a new idea on your life, a different perspective, but more precisely the observation of a change in your state of mind. Now you approach life, as when you are in love: you smile at life and your life is successful.

It is a real transformation in yourself and you have no need to think about it; you are lifted, like on a cloud. You fly from one joy to another and you fly over the hassles of existence.

Always give a part of what you have received and you put yourself in a universal movement of giving and receiving. It is time to participate in the general and almost imperceptible movement to improve our world. You have received for six months now the fruits of your commitment and you can now begin to transmit all these experiences around you and allow your loved ones to get the same benefits that were offered to you.

There is always someone around you that is sad, that is grieving, suffering and lives under a gray sky. It is to this person that you must bring your help and give him the means to bring back the sun and find the beauty of life. Immerse yourself with these laws and make it a permanent reality of your existence.

Remember that it is not what you read, but what you experience, it is not the thought but the action that transforms life.

"Reading is to eat and drink. The mind that does not read
decline as the body that does not eat."

VICTOR HUGO

We are composed of three parts, soul, mind and body. It is essential to feed these three. If you omit one, there will be deficiencies. Reading promotes the development of the mind, memory and protects against degenerative brain diseases.

Where there is ignorance judgments abound.

The powers in place have often banned books; we remember the blacklisting, the censorship or book burnings perpetrated by the Nazis. Tyrants often neglect or prevent the teaching of reading. Because the one who can read begins to know and to grow and can no longer be influenced because of ignorance or poverty of mind. To read kills ignorance and prejudice…
Keep on learning, informing yourself, developing and opening your mind: always.
Leaders read! They increase their knowledge and skills and thus know how to win.
Being a leader of your life is wanting to know and to understand your life better and being able to achieve it with grace and satisfaction.

To read a little daily increases one's wealth, not to read just accentuates one's poverty.

Practice

The purpose of life is personal development and experience. The sooner we learn the quicker we can apply the knowledge that will place our life on the best possible path.

Therefore our mind must be fed *daily* as the other two components of our being.

Your exercise will be to take the habit of reading a little every day. You are already reading this book, congratulations!

But much beyond that, you can deepen the laws addressed in this book by reading other books that develop these topics or any other topic that brings you new knowledge or understanding.

Take the habit to always have a book with you (so two with this one).

And whenever you have a moment, during a waiting period somewhere, while being on public transport, flip a few pages.

This will surely be more positive than a newspaper found here and there.

This is not because it would not be good to read a newspaper (it is always good to learn), but because this reading is rarely positive and mostly because it is not your selection of topics, while you can freely choose your book according to your desires.

"We think from what we are writing
and not the opposite."

Louis ARAGON

The power of words is to materialize your thoughts in writing. It is through writing down your thoughts that you give life to them.

Words are a force, a vibration; they act immediately and remain engraved. When you write you stimulate millions of neural connections in the brain, your thought intensifies and materializes through writing.

Always write in the present tense, considering that everything is already done, it will help the materialization of things to manifest. And write only with positive terms. Use your words wisely. Make them tell the truth and speak forcefully!

Words are strength and power! Use them accordingly to generate your creative power through them!

Practice

As of this week, in addition to your small notebook, make a habit of carrying a small notepad with you or Post-It™ and whenever you come up with ideas, words or phrases, write them down. This will allow you to forget less, because in writing you consciously activate a part of your brain. And especially materialize your thoughts. This will also give you another opportunity to reflect later on with a particular point of view to this thought that you put in writing. Try this practice for the first week, it will bring a new dimension to your mind and your projects. Then make it a good habit to get a clear mind and a sense of appropriateness.

"God gave you a gift of 86400 seconds today.
Have you used one to say "thank you"?"

William A. WARD

If we had to choose which of the fifty-two magical laws is the most important, the one that will change positively your whole life, it would undoubtedly be gratitude. The world belongs to those who know how to rejoice. By making gratitude their lifestyle, they turn it into gold. When you are filled with gratitude, you are grateful. In this state it is therefore impossible to be negative.

The more you are full of gratitude, the more you are positive and you attract positive people and situations, it is that simple. Gratitude is the permanent reflex to thank life, your life, everything that happens to you, both good experiences and not so favorable ones. As each experience makes us evolve, gratitude is ultimately always positive.
Thank for all that you have received and you will continue to receive, and thank all those who have crossed your path, your family, friends and colleagues.

At every moment life offers us gifts, it is only by being truly aware of this fact that we activate the power of gratitude. Only gratitude can create the true magic of life and cause spontaneous miracles. Whenever it comes, celebrate it, spend your day, your life thanking it. Celebrate whenever a new way of expressing gratitude manifests.

Live the magic of life and be the magician in your own life! Celebrate it like a flame swaying in the hymn of joy.

Being in an attitude of gratitude is the key to directly change your frequency into high vibration.

Practice

It is critical to understand that gratitude finds its roots in faith and to know that everything that happens to us is always perfect, that we have consciously or unconsciously created what happens to us and therefore that we can change it to our advantage.

The goal this week is to experience gratitude for each day so you can see for yourself the true power of gratitude that will transform your life almost instantly.

Say thanks at least a hundred times a day!!! (mentally or verbally according to offered opportunities) for all situations and encounters. This conditions you to find the positive in every situation and will ultimately attract only positive situations that will make you thank more.

Focus your whole week on gratitude, think only about this, if you really and truly do, you will already see significant results already after a week and you will better understand the value of applying this approach throughout the rest of your life.

> "Make your dream devour your life
> so that life does not devour your dream."
>
> Antoine de SAINT-EXUPÉRY

Often in our lives, we find that some of our dreams could not be realized and that some desires were thwarted. Yet we must never stop dreaming and believing again and again otherwise we kill our soul softly.

You made a list of your dreams and some have already been achieved, it confirms to you that this approach is effective.

You are on the right track right now, it is important not to give up because it is not going fast enough. Everything is always perfect. When your vibrational frequency is at the equivalence of your dreams, they then immediately come true.

The only thing that may prevent the materialization of your dreams is the fear of failure.

If you do not see your dreams as a goal, but just as an experience on paving your life, you will never be kept waiting.

Waiting always pushes the time and prevents realization.

As Eleanor Roosevelt said **"The future belongs to those who believe in the beauty of their dreams."**

Imagine the beauty of your dreams in beautiful colors, sounds, perfumes and sensations.

Use your five senses that will enable a better materialization thanks to the vibration of what you feel.

In fact, remember, what you **live hence feel,** emits a much more powerful wave than the simple fact of thinking.

Practice

Most people give up on their dreams when they think they do not come true right away or not in accordance with their expectations.

They then simply make do with just an offshoot of the dream, but they cannot be happy with it.

Remember that your dream comes true when your frequency is aligned with your dream; it can take you years to understand this principle and to see your approach succeed.

For example, if you want to be successful in business, you first need to have the skill, discipline and attitude of the one that you intend to become.

Very often some are waiting to achieve their goals to become what they want to be.

They therefore never do manage to become themselves before obtaining any material success.

To maintain your dream and vibrate at the same frequency, you must think enthusiastically and continuously about the achievement of your dream, throughout the day, at least ten times a day. You will thus see very quickly signs that confirm to you that you are approaching the right frequency.

"Peace is not the opposite of agitation.
It is the absence of agitation.
It is a completely relaxed state."

AMMA (MATA AMRITANANDAMAYI)

We often have a misconception about what it means
"to be at peace."
When you are at peace with yourself as you are, it does not mean
that your life is always peaceful.
This means that even in the midst of a storm, you can always
return to your heart, your greatest refuge and create calm inside
you. It is only when you are within yourself that peace is possible,
without paying attention anymore to the outside.

Let speak those who speak, let judge those who judge.

Being at peace is being happy without expecting anything from
anyone. One of the greatest masteries of life is *to be at peace with
our past in order not to ruin our present.*
Once you are at peace with yourself and your goals for your life,
nothing can affect your motivation for life, because you do not
have expectations anymore. As soon as you are at peace, it shows
on your face and your facial features change, your frequency
increases in order to attract experiences of peace and love; on the
contrary when you do not, you attract experiences of conflicts; it
is as simple as that.

Practice

Your quiet strength is your greatest balance.
Your exercise this week is to work on agitation inside you, the one that prevents your quiet strength to prevail. This agitation is always connected to the mind and not to your body here and now. It is easier to observe our body than our mind.

This week be sure to listen to your body, gestures, voice and gait. Whenever you feel stress inside your body it is because a certain agitation is manifesting inside you and prevents you from being at peace. Ask yourself the question with lightness and humor: but why I am stirred like that?
Welcome the answer quietly, but above all do not develop it. Inhale for five seconds and then exhale as long as possible by fixing your attention on the breath only; this will establish the calm in you.
Repeat this exercise until you feel your pace is slowing down.

"No external grace is complete
if the inner beauty does not enliven it.
The beauty of the soul spreads
as a mysterious light over the beauty of the body."

VICTOR HUGO

The beauty of life is all around you. Open your eyes and discover it, absorb it, appreciate it, reflect it and be part of it.
What is important is learning to see the best in the other, learning to see his heart and soul!

Too often we look at what our own eyes see and what our ears hear. If you manage to feel only with our heart what is best in the other, you not only help yourself greatly, but also you will help the other in the same momentum. To live and embody beauty you must see what is beautiful at every moment.

Be demanding with regards to the clothes you wear, places you frequent and representations of beauty. Surround yourself with pictures, paintings depicting beauty.
Eliminate from your life everything that does not represent the beauty of life. Embodying in your everyday life all that is beautiful both inside and outside will only bring beauty into your life.

Practice

The only beauty that remains while aging is the one we have developed within us. The more you develop inner beauty and kindness right now, the more you will influence your cells, which then condition all the features of your body.

To be the beauty, we must above all work our values and take care of our appearance.

Remember that we attract the beauty we represent.

If our beauty is only in appearance, we attract a superficial and ephemeral beauty.

On the other hand, if our beauty is made of true values, we will attract experiences filled with true and lasting beauty.

The exercise this week, is to every day embody the beauty in you by integrating the concepts discussed in this chapter (your values) and by experiencing the beauty at every moment.

"True simplicity combines goodness to beauty."

PLATO

"Set your sights high, the higher the better.
Expect the most wonderful things to happen,
not in the future but right now.
Realize that nothing is too good.
Allow absolutely nothing to hamper you
or hold you up in any way."

EILEEN CADDY

The purpose of life is above all about living the best possible life. No matter our successes and failures, material things, family, children, possessions, attachments or relationships...
The only "obsession" you need to have every minute of your life, it is to be well, **HERE AND NOW!**
In other words at the present moment; focus on this fundamental point all the time.

Seek excellence in all that you undertake in order to always feel good, to then be even better. Do not tolerate a state where you do not feel well. If you can avoid it, seek a thought or even better an action that will make you feel better. Respond immediately, do not wait until the next day.

If you focus your attention at every moment to always feel better, no matter what happens, you will attract through a virtuous circle situations and experiences that will make you feel better. This is one of the most important secrets to increase one's vibrational frequency and generating life situations that provide the desired happiness.
Often when we think we are well, we believe that this is normal and it is acquired and subsequently, we do not do anything to be better.

When we take something for granted we do not fight for it anymore and we end up losing it.

Tell yourself that if you are down in the pit, it is the best news that can be, because you can finally realize that you can be better and you do everything to recover.

Imagine the billions of cells that are partying in your body, laughing out loud and elated, and say the magic formula: *thank you, thank you, thank you, my dears for renewing yourselves in good health and bringing me so much joy, gratitude and well-being.*

Practice

The exercise of this week is to always feel better wherever you are. It is not about feeling good, but more especially to gradually seek to be better if you are not very well, and even better if the situation is already enjoyable.

Do not tolerate when you do not feel well.

If negative thoughts, fears or others come up, immediately look for a way to think about something else, act in a way that makes you happy. Think of it this way, without respite, and ask yourself the following question:

how do I feel now? What can I do to feel even better? You will find very quickly that your mind is always focused on being always better.

You will continue to attract situations and feelings in which you feel better and better.

"I have not failed. I have just found 10000 ways
that will not work."

Thomas EDISON

People often do not follow their goals or drop them along the way, because they are not really their own goals.

It is the others who want to transform you and not in the way you expect. The basics to achieving your objectives are to understand them. We must understand our goals and dreams.

What do you really want? And why do you want it? What will it give you when you have it?

If you know the answer to these three questions and it resonates very strongly in you, you then activate a process of self-motivation that nothing can stop. If you do not do it, the slightest annoyance will make you abandon or modify your goals. For a fruit tree to finally give its first fruits, time must be allowed for growth and maturation. If you think the barriers are temporarily annoying, try to stop just one season. If you rush things because the fruit does not come fast enough, your tree will die and all previous years will be lost. To follow your goals and achieve them, you must never give up. All you have planted is not lost, but we must maintain, continue to apply fertilizer and to believe, even if you do not see results immediately.

Do not get discouraged; *it is often the last key in the keychain that is the right one to open the door.*

It is essential to constantly remind us why we made our choice and not how our goals will be achieved.

Once the why is anchored, the how presents itself naturally.
What matters is not what is earned by completing our goals, but what we become by working to achieve them. However, do not confuse expectations and goals. One goal is for the long term expectation is conceivable only for the short term.

Waiting always provokes an impatience, the one of wanting everything as soon as possible. When it is not going the way you want, it is because you have focused your attention on expectations instead of pursuing your goals. Living with expectations prevents the achievement of your goals.

Practice

The ideal to be able to follow your goals is to write them down in your notebook.

Mark all life goals that come to mind, both the smallest ones like improvements of character, learning to follow, vacation plans, etc., and the biggest ones affecting your dreams. Make a list of at least thirty points. Then, at the beginning of each month take ten minutes to think about what happened, write off those completed, follow up the progress of others and you can continue writing down new ones.

Observe those that have evolved and visualize others, this will help you to constantly monitor your goals, to visualize their progress and will encourage you to stick to them.

> "The higher you get, the farther you see."
>
> CONFUCIUS

Humanity often seeks its salvation in angels without understanding that it is in fact itself called to grow its wings in this life.

The basic rule when a problem or a crisis occurs is not to react. Take a step back, use any excuse to save time and therefore rise above the situation. But do not react right away. Rather act when the emotional reaction settles. Always look for the bright side of the problem and rebound by acting and not reacting, it makes all the difference.

All situations always end up by improving when we let go. Nothing is ever as bad as it seems at first.
Sufferings only begin to fade when we manage to float above them.
Knowing to leave the dense material on the Earth and rise gently above the situation.

To rise above any situation is the only way to grow and understand the lessons of life.

Practice

This week, the goal is to create calm inside you and take a step back from every thought or situations that might worry you. Remember to allow the time to flow every time.

Tensions will this way dissipate and other elements be added and enable you to act with more discernment.

To help you get some perspective, you can close your eyes and visualize the conflictual situation as a stage below you, as if you were flying over it, this will help to put into perspective the situation. Picture a stage where everyone plays a role, nothing is serious.

By rising above, you will take the situation much less seriously and you will be amazed how most of the times things will improve by themselves.

"Half an hour of meditation is essential except when one's very busy. In that case one hour is necessary."

SAINT FRANÇOIS de SALES

True knowledge is silent knowledge, which comes when the mind is free, as soon as we get to silence the mind and the distractions of the mind, or at least reduce the flow of thoughts. Getting to silence in oneself can take years, but it is the key to start the path to inner peace and knowledge. The majority of people are controlled by their thoughts instead of controlling their own thoughts and therefore their future.

Remember, we become what we think about most often. Meditation is also to learn to integrate new thoughts that will form a new reality. Meditation is to be fully aware of the present moment, being 100% in your body and in the physical consciousness, not in the mind.

Meditation offers a great opportunity against the aging of our cells and our spirit. It allows us to obtain unrivaled health. Meditation is the key to increase one's awareness.

Practice

If up to now you have never meditated, this is the exact right moment to start.

From now on, you will strive to be less in the head in order to be in the heart. This way your vibration level will lift to a higher frequency. There are many ways to meditate, using sounds, practicing different breathing techniques, working in various positions, mantras, prayers, etc. You can start to investigate by asking around you about the most suitable technique for you. But first, here is one quite simple and very effective to use every day for ten minutes.

Lie down or sit in a comfortable position.

Put a relaxing music at a moderate volume level.

Close your eyes and focus your attention only on your breathing, inhale air with the nose up from the stomach slowly for seven seconds by pushing it up to the center of the chest, then hold the air for three seconds and exhale the air through the mouth and down back into the stomach, as if it evacuates through the navel. This simple exercise will increase your ability to focus on the heart and will bring you a great relaxation.

"Let us rise up and be thankful,
because if we did not learn a lot
at least we learnt a little,
and if we did not learn a little,
at least we did not get sick,
and if we got sick,
at least we did not die;
so, let us all be thankful."

BUDDHA (Siddhārtha GAUTAMA)

In order to receive you must agree to receive, be aware and grateful that you constantly receive, even if it is not exactly as you might hope for now.

You receive according to what you allow yourself to receive and your belief that you can get everything you ask. Welcome, accept and celebrate all the little things in life that you receive each day, be immensely happy for that, thank and thank again, and these things will become increasingly important.

As long as you live, you receive from life and it is already the most precious gift.

Practice

To receive continuously, gratitude is one of the major keys. It is often said that those who know how to accept gifts get more than others.

The exercise this week is to be responsive to every moment of the day, to all that you get.

Start with what is vital but unnoticed.

First enjoy and rejoice yourself of the air you breathe and the daylight you see and expand your awareness of the gifts that you were given to the most significant elements: to be valid, to have a job, people who appreciate you, friendship, someone who loves you, an expression of sympathy; you easily find out that one day fills us in with gifts.

The important thing is the awareness of being receptive.

The only fact to take gifts for naturally granted depreciates anything you can receive.

If you take for granted being healthy and therefore you do nothing to maintain it; if it seems to you superfluous to thank for this wonderful gift, it will not be long before you get sick. This rule applies to everything else. Being receptive means being in harmony with all other laws, to listen, to thank observing everything that you continuously receive. In your small notebook that you always carry with you, write throughout the day what you receive saying: thank you, thank you and thank you!!!

This will allow you to be even more aware and thus to continuously receive.

What are your progress?

Now that you see the changes that have occurred over the last three months, you may have found out that you now are beyond the notions of positive and negative, as you can appreciate things at their true value.

Without any effort in will-power or thought, you manage to be peaceful and perfectly balanced. A feeling of well-being is settled inside you. These past few weeks have transformed your life and opened your heart. Take the time to enjoy all the changes in you, observe the points that allow you to light up your life and pursue your dream. Focus particularly on what brings beauty in life and allows you to always be better. You understood that you can open the door to abundance and that you have to follow your aim to achieve your dream.

The coming weeks will be devoted to the exercise of living here and now, seeing farther, raising your consciousness and always finding your right place. Sincerity and determination will help you pursue your goals.

You have known for long that love and the actions dictated by the heart are the keys of life. But these easy and powerful exercises will help you understand these great lessons of life using empathy and respect.

You must always take care of yourself, to be present and available for others. You have noticed considerable progress because you are already not the same anymore. You see people stare at you, cite you as a role model and want to be like you. You are becoming much better than you were and you are getting closer and closer to your ideal.

Apply-yourself, exercise every day in joy. You are doing like this just for yourself, for your own good, to be in control of your life.

"The most important moment is the present
because if we do not take care of our present
we miss our future."

Bernard WERBER

Most people seek their happiness in the memories or in a "hypothetical future" instead of living their happiness in the present. Living in the present is to turn your back to the past, keep your eyes open toward the future while keeping your feet on the ground, intensely in the present moment.

Do not lose your precious time anymore with rumors, relics of the past, negative thoughts or things out of your control. Invest your energy in the positive present. In the present we always feel good. This is when we connect our mind to the past with all regrets, or future with all the anxieties born of ignorance, that we do not have any more space to feel good. The true present moment must be devoid of any spirit or reflection, like when you breathe; you just do it, without asking yourself any questions.

You simply *are*; this is what it is living in the present moment.

It is when you realize that you are not present that you become present.

It is only by being fully aware of the present moment that we can build our future.

The only true time is the present moment, *if you focus on a time that has already happened or not happened yet, you are out of time.*

Never wait for the right time to live you want to live, never wait the right time to say I love you to those you love, never wait for the right time to do the things you need to do; because the right time is now, only you have the power to get things done and to decide when it is the right time. When we wait, we push back the time, we push back life and then we regret what we did not dare to do.

Practice

To live in the present moment, remember this motto: **"Less mind for more physical.".**
If your mind is wandering around, it is because you detach yourself from the present moment. So you decrease your chances of better materializing the reality of what you undertake. The practice you are about to start as of this week is a little trick that immediately brings you back into the present moment. Whenever you are too controlled by your thoughts, say aloud – **"Stop!"** and take awareness of your five senses.
 Start with your eyes; looking like a child that is discovering everything around him. Listen to the sounds that surround you at this moment. Use your sense of touch, make contact with an object and realize fully what is your feeling.
Activate your sense of taste by drinking or eating something, or simply by swallowing your saliva and then pay attention to the smells around you.
This very quick little exercise will give you the advantage of focusing immediately on the present moment.
Practice it as much as possible during the day, whenever you feel the need.

"Insanity is doing the same thing over and over again and expecting different results."

Albert EINSTEIN

It is only by learning that we evolve and can change things.

If you always do what you have always done you will always get what you have always got.

How could one imagine for only one second otherwise? As indicated at the beginning of the book, if you want things to change, you must first change yourself and then things will change!

But for things to change you must have a willingness to learn at the highest level, want to learn all the time, even the little things and challenge yourself; it is the basic key.

What man does not want to learn through wisdom, he will learn it by suffering going through negative experiences that will keep reproducing as long as he has not learnt the lessons to give himself a new impetus.

To learn you have to observe, listen, open your mind to novelty and change. A famous quote from Confucius says:

"When you do not want to learn anymore, you die!".

The secret of eternal youth, of centenarians, beyond a positive attitude in life is the desire to learn a new thing every day.

Our body is composed of approximately ten billion cells. Every day millions of them die and the same numbers are renewed.

As soon as we do not want to learn anymore, we give them this information.

So they can only renew themselves in a morbid way and therefore will work against life.

When we think we know everything it is that we know nothing. When we finally realize this; it is the beginning of the great learning.

Life is beautiful; we learn so much every day. This is the greatest wealth; we often understand later on what we believed we had already understood. Listening to what life shows us is really learning life.

Practice

In order to build ourselves the best possible life, we always need to work on our basics, as long as it is not acquired we repeat the same mistakes bigger and bigger.

This week you become a child again, who is curious to learn and observe everything.

Ask yourself this question:

What can teach me this experience? This situation?

What can I learn today? In an hour?

In addition to this book and the others that you already read (because you already experienced reading in week 27), this week you will manage to get a new book that will help you to learn something else in connection with the fifty-two laws or a skill that you feel the need to deepen.

"The purpose of life is to give amusement,
and if life is too lazy for this,
there is nothing left but to
help it along a little."

Milan KUNDERA

Like what you do and do what you like.

All what you do must be fun somehow. To have fun does not mean that you should not do things seriously, but with a smile and lightness. Always look for joy in what you do. For what seems still impossible today, change your attitude and it will become possible. Reject everything that is not pleasant, rewarding, enjoyable or beautiful.

Experience the happiness now. We often see the importance of things only when we lose them. A human being struggles to perceive if he has not experienced deprivation. When we have fun doing things, as children do, we live completely in the present moment. This allows us to forget all the hassles of life and recharges our batteries.

This way, all activities, even the most demanding ones, are then achieved in such a simple way that we wonder why we did not have this attitude before...

Practice

This is the week where you will have even more fun.
You have to get up every day saying:
"Am I, at this moment, bored or having fun?"
If your activity does not give you the freedom to have fun (as often repetitive activities of daily life), you can still rejoice about it anyway. In that case look for something to sweeten your day as decorating a part of your environment: improving the appearance of your office with decorations will make you smile or give you the impression to have fun. Putting some music on, if you can, helps a lot.
Bid farewell to someone, this way:

"Be well and have a lot of fun!"

Have a lot of fun this week.

"If someone says: "it is killing me to make you understand"
let him die."

JACQUES PRÉVERT

If you want to learn to know someone, watch the way he/she communicates with you, beyond words, knowledge and reason.

You will learn much more than you can imagine. It is are not the people that speak better than others that have the best things to say; to communicate, it is above all being able to listen to others, to give them the space to express themselves, to welcome what they expose and then take your turn to express yourself in this same reciprocity. Communicating is not trying to be right, it is to hear what the other expresses.

Communicate only with your heart, feelings and responsibly; your words will be then more powerful and true.
The power of silence is the strength of those knowing best how to communicate. In silence, you learn by listening to the other and prepare what you are going to say with much more wisdom than if you talk continuously.

It is crucial to control the verb i.e. your speech, because it has a great influence on your vibration. To communicate is not to keep rancor within oneself.

It is about saying what needs to be said at the right time to stay completely free. Communicate as much as possible with reasoning and reflection, but please communicate!
It always avoids misunderstandings.

It is thanks to the magic of the encounters with people of exception that hearts can vibrate in a nice frequency... so always be exceptional!

Practice

Learn to communicate even better this week.

You do it by observing and listening to others. As soon as you communicate with your heart, your voice changes, it is more profound and true. With the simple tone of voice of a person we can learn more about his vibration, health and sincerity.

Take time to observe the ones who speak, to try to understand their attitude beyond words and gestures and then analyze it for yourself, looking at how you can improve your voice, body language and communication.

And with this new learning, communicate as much as possible throughout the week, but that does not mean of course to speak more.

"The problem is not to think big or small,
but to see the big picture."

CLAUDE LELOUCH

Vision leads to nothing, unless it is combined with action.

It is not enough to look at the top of the mountain, but we must start to climb it step by step.

Vision is your most ardent, deepest and most cherished desires. Positive projections are the ones that you make from your life and projects. Without vision, your thoughts are struggling a lot to materialize. To get closer to your dreams and desires you have to see them properly and be able to anticipate your rejoicing. To experiment them straight away, start to gather the images and experiences related to them. We attract what we project, visualize with our heart and believe is going to happen!

To have vision is to have faith that sooner or later, our dreams will come true and accept whatever arises, even the unexpected, because there is always a reason for it to happen.
You have to make your vision vibrate, live it, rejoice as if you are already living it; the more you are in this attitude the more it manifests, while knowing to let go and entrust your greatest desires.
To see the big picture by having this vision to seize the best for you is to trust your life and your ability to make it perfect.

Practice

You still have your list of dreams and desires that you have elaborated the first weeks and that you continue to read every day in the morning and evening (see Law No.1).

This week, move as close as possible to your visions so that they really appear. If your vision is not felt deep within you with feelings and emotions, it will remain an intellectual concept, not vibrated and with little chance of being materialized. This is the key to turn your visions into reality. Cut out pictures of items you wish to purchase and display them.

Browse holiday catalogs, try on the clothes that you wish to obtain, visit the places where you want to live, hang out with people who are what you want to be or represent the success that you desire to have.

What you visualized will come to you sooner or later.

"Great thoughts come from the heart."

VAUVENARGUES (Luc de CLAPIERS, Marquis de)

It is only your thoughts that shape your reality and attract all your life experiences. We are what we think and what we are is the result of the sum of our thoughts. *You are not your thoughts, but the one who choose them.*

Negative thoughts attack the body and mind. They are the first symptoms of the disease.

We must begin by curing the mind to then heal our body.

Powerful thoughts must release immediately feeling of strength and absolute well-being. When you have a powerful thought, you feel good. This is the criterion; it is as simple as that.

Powerful thoughts make you stronger and raise you. It is only the great thoughts that make great men and create prosperity.

Think big; think big all the time!

Every day we have about 50,000 thoughts. You may not think 50,000 times in a day about what you want, but try not to think at least 50,000 times about what worries or disturbs you, because at the end of the day what we believe most often we eventually attract.

Practice

Remember that when your thoughts are positive and powerful you feel good and you attract people and similar experiences.

To put power in our thoughts, we should be more aware of our negative thoughts, those lowering vibrations, and eliminate them. Any thoughts dominated by fear or causing a feeling of anxiety is precisely not a powerful thought, it can help you identify those pushing down your frequency and prevent powerful thoughts from staying with you.

This week focus your attention mainly on the words you use, say or read and on most of your emitted thoughts. Feel invincible with your thinking.

Only you have the power to authorize the thoughts you choose to develop your life.

Only use words and sentences, powerful and positive (e.g. selected words in the exercise of the law No. 20), and others that will allow you to feel great and full of joy.

"One can escape everything but one's conscience."

Stefan ZWEIG

The major purpose of the evolution of humanity is its personal development; raising its consciousness should only concern, which will lead to its salvation.

Raising one's consciousness is increasing one's vibration.
You will never be able to pass on a pessimistic point of view to a person who has a high frequency.

Raising one's consciousness is developing one's own spirituality; a higher consciousness is obviously spiritual, whatever one's beliefs.

Favor every day all that is positive in nature, in your readings, movies, music you listen to, your friends and especially the thoughts you allow to enter your mind.
Avoid at all cost lower energies, those who do not make us feeling well and those we do not take instant awareness of, but will decrease our energy over the medium term. Walk away in silence from negative people, bull-headed or bellicose, without fuss. The continuous attention you pay to negative events, unhappy people and negative information, favors their unduly presence in your life experience.
To have a high level of consciousness is to perceive and distinguish the lower frequencies.

Raising consciousness is done through empathy and respect for all living beings regardless of their beliefs or origins.

Practice

Raise one's consciousness is thus enhancing one's values. This includes perceiving all outlooks with love, respecting life and humanity, being vigilant about anything that harms them: food, environment and even toxic thoughts.
This week focus your thinking on your spirituality and mission on Earth.

Why are you here, where are you?

Think hard about it before sleeping at night asking for messages and answers in your dreams; or any other signs that could help you. Bear in mind that a high consciousness without a minimum of spirituality is almost impossible. Look for this spirituality in you that speaks to you and sounds true.
If you have not yet developed it, orient yourself in the coming months with readings that will favor your personal development in this direction.

"Every individual has three character structures:
the one he has, the one he shows,
and the one he believes to have."

ALPHONSE KARR

Sincerity is an unending effort to follow one's soul as it is.
Being honest with yourself is to avoid cheating with others.
The most difficult challenge is to be ourselves in a world where
everyone is trying to make us become someone else!
To be sincere, is to speak without disguising one's thoughts. Too
many people live an unauthentic life defined by others and a
system, often to be recognized or accepted.

**However, self-acceptance is the key element of well-being
and positive emotions.**

Accepting yourself first is the way to accept and receive other
more easily.
If there is one kind of person one must absolutely be wary of, it
is the genuine fake.
Words are fine, but only acts consistent with them give real
answers.
When we are sincere, we act with the heart, our feelings, and
therefore in accordance and alignment with what we are.
It is only in the sincerity of our actions that our connection to
the power to create the thought of reality becomes then possible.

Practice

The law of attraction returns to you the exact attitude you have towards yourself and others. If you are real and in accordance with yourself, others will be real with you.
This week think about this principle.
For every action you make, every important thought you have, ask yourself:

- *Am I in accordance with myself?*
- *Am I real and authentic?*
- *Is this action in line with my way of thinking?*
- *Do I feel good?*

This week, being sincere as often as possible in everything you do, you take the best path to really start living in the heart.

"The truest wisdom is a resolute determination."

Napoléon BONAPARTE

In life there is no obstacle, just paths that must be explored in a different way...

When a door is closing, it is great news, because at the same time there is always another one that is opening, but we cannot see it because we stayed behind the other door, so it is the best moment to be determined to move forward differently.

It is in the moments of decision making that your destiny is shaped. The intention and firmness that you put in all that you undertake is fundamental and just confirms that you are aligned and thus in accordance with your thoughts. Seize the opportunities!

Do not wait for the Perfect Moment. Take the moment as it is and make it perfect. There is a small step between can and cannot. To take this step can totally change your destiny. This decision made in one second can change a whole life.
When you are determined, you do not care about the opinion of others and you take action!!!

Not to depend on the opinion of others is to be determined and to move forward. Have the full power of your determination on each of your actions and your goals will be materialized much more easily.

Practice

This week exercise yourself to give strength to your thoughts. The determination will carry you to the outcome of an action or decision. Even if you change your mind later, put emphasis on this determination. It will empower your mind whatever happens. The strength of intention makes all the difference against an intention not followed by a firm determination. Exercise yourself, even in small things in life, be determined, do not hesitate and go for it!

You will understand very quickly that by acting with determination in everything you do, you will increase your charisma and the results of your actions.

> "Health is not just the absence of a disease.
> It is an inner joyfulness that should be ours
> all the time; a state of positive well-being."
>
> DEEPAK CHOPRA

As mentioned earlier we are composed of three parts, the soul, body and mind, so it is imperative to "feed" the three parts of our being, if one is missing, there will be a deficiency. Remember: as soon as we feel good, our vibration is high and we attract positive experiences.

A healthy body gives a healthy mind and a healthy mind favors a healthy body. *Mens sana in corpore sano*, ancients already knew the matter well. To feel good within ourselves, which favors all that creates life in our mind and body, and to raise our consciousness: is to vibrate and give information to our cells of a good physical and mental condition by eliminating or at least reducing all that does not favor it.

One of the secrets to avoid putting on weight: think light! Is the way we feed ourselves determines our way of thinking...
The more you expand the goodness and love within your body, the more it will be visible outside; and each year some part of you will rejuvenate.

Disease: do not worry, but treat it!

Practice

We have been developing a lot during the past weeks about everything that affects thoughts and spirit, but when the body does not follow the spirit cannot rise.

The maintenance of the body depends on the quality of your diet. Favoring natural products instead of processed foods will have a huge impact on your health. Maintaining your body is dependent on being aware of your environment, the pollutants, the medications you are on and all that does not favor life, your life! Maintaining your body cannot be done without proper physical exercise. Without exercise, the energy does not circulate properly. The organism needs at least one to two hours of intense activity (brisk walking for half an hour, climbing stairs) or sports a week.

Practice a sport or exercise that you enjoy, but that makes you sweat and increases your heart rate. The cardio training provides better brain oxygenation, nutrients transported throughout the body and toxin elimination. This activity will inevitably increase your lifespan.

Do not neglect simple and healthy activities such as cycling, swimming, walking that require little or no equipment and are easy to practice alone or with a group. So this week focus your attention on your body and how to maintain it as best as possible by giving yourself a healthy environment and consuming products that favor your quality of life. And most importantly, if you do not have an activity that makes you move, find one! Invite a friend to keep you company which will help you to commit to it. Physical activity should be fun, enjoyable: check with people around you to find out what suits you. And remember to always practice a sport or physical activity with fun so that you can practice it for a long time!

"Unhappy am I because this has happened to me.
- Not so, but happy am I, though this has happened to me,
because I continue free from pain,
neither crushed by the present nor fearing the future."

MARCUS AURELIUS

If you do not know where you are going, you will end up somewhere else.
But do not look for yourself too much, because by dint of searching you will end up getting lost.

To be at the right place at the right time with the right people is the key to success. In life, we must know how to understand what our priorities are and consequently make the right choices. We have the power to take the right path and be at the center of our lives. We also can look ahead on the road and wait for the next turn; it is only a matter of choice. But the important thing is not where we are, but our state of mind and to always be where we feel good.
As soon as our mind is in order and at the right place, we always find our place.

Chance does not exist, at every moment we are exactly at the place where our thoughts and vibrational frequency have guided us; it is then always worth it to analyze : "why am I at this exact spot now?".

What should I understand? What can I do to change this situation in my favor?

Practice

This week you will always be at the right place, at ease wherever you are. For this, use your requests and prayers. The more you are aware of being at the right place with the right people at the right time, the more you will produce the appropriate situations!

Look everywhere you go for the best place that suits you. You will know what is your place, simply be honest with yourself, love and seek the best for yourself in any situation.

Thanks up there: thank you, thank you, thank you for allowing me to be at the right place at the right time and with the right people.

ALMOST TWELVE MONTHS...

During the last past months you have noticed the importance of gratitude and goodness in your life. Reading and writing have deeply enriched you and allowed you to materialize your thoughts.

Peace and beauty are finally now part of your life, you step back from the obstacles and live better and better, because your goals are well understood.

You maintain your dream and abundance is offered. The access to your spirituality opens you to unknown worlds and you never stop learning about yourself, others and life.

Commit yourself each time, with feeling and determination to the practice of the law that is proposed. Review your notes regularly and stories of your experiences. They help to realize the evolution you have achieved.

For some time now, people around you have noticed that you have changed and this comforts you in the path you have chosen. Very often you are asked the reason for this change. You can in full consciousness invite them to discover the fifty-two magic laws that can change life.

The next laws that will be proposed give you the keys to control your emotions and feelings. You will learn to use the power of your thought while awakening. This year of self-realization will of course end up with love.

However, once you have completed the reading of this book, you can continue to use all of its laws, because living a full, complete, generous and rich life is the occupation of each moment as long as the breath brings oxygen and that the heart beats.

This book can be like your personal "Bible", you can keep on referring to it at every moment of your life because you know its power. Continuously, regardless of the type of event that you encounter, you can find answers to questions that you ask yourself, because you know its scope and you have experienced its laws through your entire being. You will always receive benefit and satisfaction from it; and it is an integral part of yourself.

Enjoy every moment, hold on, there are still a lot of dreams to fulfill, a lot of people and worlds to explore, a lot of love to give and a lot of hope to disseminate.

> "One can feel an idea
> as one feels an emotion."
>
> JIM JARMUSCH

A life with cravings is to be A-LIVE!

Be yourself and say what you feel; because those that are disturbed by this much are less important than those who do not mind. When you take action using your feelings, it is the heart that guides you and not your head. The only way of life that is worth exploring is the one of the heart.

As soon as you follow your feelings, you are in the physical and not the mental. Being aware of the present moment is the only way to create the future you desire. To be in the physical feelings, listen to all your senses simultaneously and as often as possible. You will return immediately in the present moment.

All depressions are caused by the reversal of these things. Always remember this formula, it will be a great help every time:

MORE PHYSICAL FOR LESS MIND.

Practice

Your feelings are your intuition and guide in life. It is by learning to listen more and more that you will be less and less wrong. No feeling, no emotion is mind's matter; we live with and by the heart. This week review what you felt deep within yourself. How do your experiences resonate inside you? And how can you implement all the techniques discussed in the previous chapters?

Keep this phrase in you, for each situation:

Do I take action with my heart or with what is dictated to me by reason and my head?

If you need to think about this it is that you are already not into feelings any more.

"The spirit is difficult to master and unstable.
It runs where it wants. It is a good thing to dominate it.
The tamed spirit ensures happiness."

BUDDHA (SIDDHĀRTHA GAUTAMA)

Negative emotions are responsible for the vast majority of diseases. They cause an immediate drop in the immune system and thus open the door to disease.

Worrying is refocusing attention on what we do not want.

True self-control is the control of one's fears and emotions. Do not react to adversity or aggression does not mean that you are weak, but only that you are mature enough to understand that anger and emotional reactions do not solve anything. The emotion is often rooted in fears and mind but not in the present moment.
Remember yourself the formula: "Act instead of react.".

To what you resist the most is actually what you are attracted to the most and you is also perhaps intended for you… , think about it.

Practice

Should there be one of the key points to work on in the personal development of everyone, it is really to learn to control one's emotions.

The emotional upheaval, chaos caused by their too strong reactions, are the cause of all the conflicts and degradation of the body and mind. To consciously create a positive emotion is wonderful, on the contrary to get carried away by drifting emotions always blackens the sky of life.

This week focus your attention on all the emotions that you experience throughout day and night. It is very easy to learn to decode and thus modify the emotions that are bad for you. This approach is simply your welfare indicator.

Again and again:

What sensation do you have when you feel the emotion? Good or bad? Do I feel joy, freedom, love, passion, enthusiasm, happiness or hope; or boredom, disappointment, discouragement, jealousy, hatred, fear or anger?

If you do not feel well, it is beautiful, you just have identified an emotion that will lower your energy; say immediately to yourself: STOP!

And put your attention on the emotion caused by the reverse situation, when you feel good and happy.

Think of it as long as possible, until the negative emotion disappears.

"For every minute you are angry you lose sixty seconds of happiness."

RALPH WALDO EMERSON

> "The true birthplace is where we had
> for the first time an intelligent look at ourselves."
>
> Marguerite YOURCENAR

To wake up to then awaken ourselves is to become aware of who we are, what we want out of life and what we do not want anymore.

Waking up is to find faith again in a bigger source than ourselves, to trust knowing how surrender to it, to get help from the higher dimension of our being and the Universe.

The majority of humanity is asleep, drugged, manipulated by the system and beliefs; it is a fact, alas.
It is only when you have high consciousness and spirituality and understand that YOU have the power to create your life as you want it; and that everything that happens to you is just the result of your thoughts.

To raise our consciousness is to change the settings of our mind!

If we want outstanding results, we must be in an extraordinary mood.

Your actions, new way of thinking and attitude can change while being aware that you are waking up and one thing leading to another will lead you to your awakening.

Practice

It will be a year next week that this book follows your daily life and that you assiduously practice the exercises.

Many changes have occurred in your life because you have applied these recipes.

Your level of consciousness and your openness to change have been modified through this practice, like never before.

Your quality of life has improved, you cannot turn back and you do not want that, you are close to permanent wakefulness.

You are no longer under the influence of others and any system that would like to control you.

You are free to think, want and create.

Your exercise this week is to review each chapter one by one to make sure they are well learnt.

You will develop your secret code, a personal code.

In order to do this, write on a piece of paper, your ten favorite laws, the ones you can not get rid of, those that fully define you and constitute the goal you have chosen to fully enrich your life.

As these laws have become the primary component of your existence, you will continue to apply them in every moment of your life.

"Live by the golden rule:
treat everyone the way
you want to be treated."

WAYNE HUFFMAN

A smiling heart is a heart that lives.

It is not love that gives happiness, but it is to be happy that gives love.

People do not love you for your possessions, your title or your accomplishments, they can enjoy the property you own and be impressed, but that does not mean they love you.

When you are just yourself, with authentic relationships, you are loved for what you ARE and not what you DO.

If an enemy takes up more space in your mind than a friend in your heart it is because there is something wrong with your way of thinking and the part that is "Being Love" is not vibrating as it should.

It is as if, in your garden, you are watering weeds, rather than roses! Choose well what you want... Choose to be Love for each of your heart beats in inhaling and exhaling this beautiful love wave all around you.

There are external signs of wealth and there are external signs of love. When the external signs of love manifest themselves, the luxury of life surpasses all wealth.

To live in the path of the heart in a state of consciousness is to make one's internal sun vibrating so strongly that shadow has no reason to be anymore. The light of every conscious person can influence the world.

Practice

What do you risk by being a sweetheart with all the people you meet? May be simply to do good around you and be loved even more.

As they say, the way to be a sweetheart can not be learnt in books, but in life by the experience of the heart.

The exercise of this last week is just to think about this law every day on every occasion:

Be Love! Be Love in all your interactions with others, think a hundred times a day about this mantra:

I am Love, I am Love, I am Love and all my acts are filled with love.

"I have found that if you love life, life will love you back."

ARTHUR RUBINSTEIN

The 53rd law...

<blockquote>
« But this is another story... »

Rudyard KIPLING
</blockquote>

This book you have just given yourself or you may be lucky enough to have received it as gift, had already granted you a positive move in your personal development...

With the first issue of the 52 magical laws which highlighted the extraordinary experiences and the wonderful achievements of players, the 53rd law was finally rediscovered...
It helps make things more concrete and multiply exponentially all the positive aspects of our lives.

It goes beyond the gratitude and joy together, it is the law by snowball effect that makes your world a better place and therefore the one of others.

Each person that follow the program of the 52 Magic Laws will be revealed by this 53rd law and may thus used it to achieve a greater dimension of life.

The 53rd law

The human experience of the 53rd law is a great surge of solidarity that is done TOGETHER!

Stay tuned on the latest news and developments on:

www.magiclaws.com

YOUR CODE IS NAMED AFTER THE LAWS OF YOUR LIFE!

Now you have been practicing for a whole year the lessons of these fifty-two essential laws.

You have noticed significant changes in the way you live, think and apprehend the world and love. Your life is happier; you regularly have more beneficial meetings. Your life has been enriched in every sense. Among these laws, you have freely chosen the ones that suit you, that define you, that you can trust and which you can rely on at any time. Using these laws, you have established your personal code, like no other one, because it is only effective for your personality, own feelings and experiences. The ten laws you have chosen are only yours. They will guide every act, every thought and every decision of every moment of your life.

They will **become your reason to live and your lifestyle.** This means your strictly personal way to experience life and live with your own feelings. You can refer to it without difficulty in every important moment of your life. You can meditate and think about these ten laws and mottos, because these are the ones that guide your life.

Now that you have defined your code, you can continue to do the exercises every day even more easily, every moment since they are no longer exercises but have become your lifestyle.

After understanding and applying these magic laws, your life has evolved greatly and this in only one year. Remember, your thinking and life only twelve months back. The purpose of life is above all our personal development, whatever our acquisitions, relationships, health; what matters is what we are going to become thanks to it.

When we begin this journey of personal development, we cannot go back anymore, so things will change forever for the better.
I encourage you to rejoice with life, again and again, and continue with joy your wonderful life path.
And remember one thing: the best is yet to come.

Let your life be the dream life you have always dreamed of!

Life is like a big high-speed train that passes by in front of us. In this train there are all opportunities of life, friendly and loving, dating business opportunities, the thoughts of wisdom and conscience that we capture for our development and good evolution.

All these opportunities are just passing through and often very soon, if we do not catch them, we miss and others seize them by the flight (even in the train):
• There are the ones still waiting for the train and that are resistant to anything that can change something in their life (it is in general, the fear to fail that is the obstacle);
• There are the ones that do not even see the train and wonder what we are talking about;
• There are the ones taking the next train, but most life opportunities that were in the first train are not there anymore; so they are going to drown their sorrows in the diner car of the train with a few glasses of alcohol;
• And there are the ones jumping on the train, even if they are not sure that it will go to the right destination, but they do not resist, they know that the trip will be worth it, whatever the experience.

Because what the real wealth of life is precisely the experience, even with the crisis, no one can ever steal it from us.

Acknowledgements

There are so many people that have crossed my path in life and enriched me that it would be impossible to thank them all, each personally.

I first give all my gratitude to my parents, who were able to give me during the necessary time all their love and values, my maternal grandmother, who gave me so much love and attention, my two wonderful sons, who always supported me in my work, the mother of my children and my sister.

To all my dear friends (ladies and gentlemen), who have always encouraged me to finish this book I had started writing in bits and pieces, many years ago; without them, this book would not exist, I am immensely grateful to them.

To you my friend Olivier Lebesson-Koyama, who with your talent and help managed to revise my book and give it a better shape.

And to you Nicolas Kuhn, who has done a remarkable job for the formatting of the second French edition and the translation to create the English edition (with the precious help of Michelle Macdonald for final revision).

A special thanks to all my students, who often became friends later on, who followed me for years; and through our discussions, our friendships have inspired me greatly to create all of these texts and laws that have made this book. And finally, I will never forget all the masters, healers and teachers that have crossed my path and taught me so much, as well as all these great thinkers and writers that are part of our human and intellectual heritage and have provided inspiration at every moment for our personal development.

ABOUT THE AUTHOR

Olivier Honsperger was born in Switzerland. He lived the first part of his childhood in the countryside near Geneva. He was fortunate enough to receive from his parents, both teachers, values of life and love that enabled him to make his way with as much assets as possible. Since his childhood, he was attracted to anything mystical and being very intuitive he would have the vision of events were to occur or could feel certain particular situations. At 15 years old, his life took a major turn after the death of his parents in a car accident. Very soon, by necessity, he had to move from adolescence to adulthood. His new responsibilities and raising spiritual awareness to face the events of life quickly forged his personality. So at a very young age he went to live in Paris alone, as if, life was going so fast, he felt he needed to do a thousand things at once.

For several years, he studied audio-visual realization and began his professional activity in the field of cinema and the making of commercials. It was then he felt the need to return to Geneva to resume his studies he had abandoned when leaving for Paris.

Once he received his BA in International Management, he began his entrepreneurship, in marketing, sales and paramedic sales. It was during this period that he met his future wife with whom he was married for twelve years. Two wonderful and loving sons were born of this union.

At the age of 25, he was the head of a large company that he had developed between Paris and Geneva in the music and mobile telephony industries. This company provided work to thousands of independent sellers; he had a lot of fun training and helping them to succeed. However his work in personal development work brought him during this period, more fun activity than the excitement, exercising his business. After reorganization with new partners, the human values that made the success of his company were replaced by greed, contrary to the logic of sharing and respect of the values he had established. It is at this moment that another important turning point occured in his life. He realized that he was not comfortable in his role and he was not really doing what he wanted. Finally, he felt that he was drifting away from his quest, soul path and personal development. He then decided to stop everything, right in the middle of the expansion of his business. He subsequently lost everything he had earned by his own choice; he even filed for personal bankruptcy. It was for him a new opportunity to start afresh and to devote himself to what was close to his heart.

He trained with various specialists in both physical and mental health and created his own school in Geneva and trained more than five hundred Reiki masters, becoming a reference in the field. Diplomas obtained at the school allow health practitioners to be recognized by the health insurance companies.

In 2006, he published simultaneously two books "Terre aujourd'hui" ("Earth today") and "Terre demain" ("Earth tomorrow"), in which he communicated his passion for life and the essence of his heart approach, which is to bring more welfare to those that he met. The means he used were multiple, as on top of the books he had published, he published audio coaching methods, he gave lectures and continued to provide medical cares.

For nearly twenty years, the strength of his teaching comes from both his sensitivity and heart qualities, but also his experience as an entrepreneur. He always combines a sensitive and emotional approach, with a pragmatic and practical practice.

The fundamental intent that guides him is to provide a spiritual and non-dogmatic opening to enable everyone to achieve a higher level of awareness and control over their lives.

For him, the only purpose of our time on earth is solidarity toward everybody and personal development to be in harmony with oneself.

This new approach that offers fifty-two magical laws to transform your life, is the perfect illustration of this statement.

TABLE OF CONTENTS

Magic Life Academy
Coach training in MLL (Magic Laws of Life)

You have read and practiced the lessons of this book and you were impressed by the power of the Magical Law of Life. They have made a real transformation in your way of life and your relationship to others.

You can now make out of it a career in harmony with your thinking.

These laws are universal laws of life which each of us experiences indirectly every day without being automatically aware of it.

Because we use these lessons when we work at our personal development and when we pay attention to others.

Healthcare workers, social workers, teachers and more generally all those that are related to helping others use them every day. These people, whether they are therapists or simply have a philanthropic approach, are using already proven and serious methods.

However, these methods require in general a long learning process. The approach and teaching of the Magic Laws of Life (MLL) is compatible with all these methods, but represent a coaching technique with a universal vocation.

They involve everyone, to address all life situations. This means that anyone can apply them.

Parents can integrate them to develop the best education for their children. Individuals can use it in all approaches related to human interactions. In professional relationships: executives or managers can better manage their teams and get a better performance in their activities.

The MLL is accessible to everyone because it only requires a heart commitment and an open mind. If you are one of those people whose daily life is based on mutual support and the dedication, or are simply caring for those they rub shoulders with; you will find in the training of MLL coach new opportunities in your life and way to make your generous ideals come true by making the MLL your new work, or by enriching your current activity with this contribution, which will allow you to be more efficient, practical and fast paced in your business.

Likewise, already experienced therapists can expand their business and open themselves to new situations and audiences. The coach training in MLL includes all coaching principles already proven, but to practice them is very simple and they can be integrated quickly and sustainably.

Practices you already use in your personal development can be perfectly integrated into the MLL to work in greater depth on some topics.

Magic Life Academy has developed a training program over a year supported by renowned professionals including distance learning and practical training.

It offers educational support adapted to today's world using interactive technologies and a certification opening up on new horizons.

INFORMATION : **WWW.MAGICLAWS.COM**

www.ingramcontent.com/pod-product-compliance
Lightning Source LLC
LaVergne TN
LVHW022011080426
835513LV00009B/672